André Gide
and the
Art of Autobiography

André Gide
and the
Art of Autobiography:
A Study of
Si le grain ne meurt

C.D.E. Tolton

MACMILLAN OF CANADA
MACLEAN-HUNTER PRESS

ISBN 0-7705-1251-8

Printed in Canada for

The Macmillan Company of Canada Limited
70 Bond Street
Toronto M5B 1X3

Contents

Introduction

MOST people who become at all seriously interested in either the life or the art of André Gide read *Si le grain ne meurt* very early in their studies. Yet among Gide's well-known works, it has attracted relatively little scholarly attention. Critics have tended to use it as a helpful source for biographical information, but have stayed clear of either synthesizing its history or analysing its artistry. The present study is, first of all, an attempt to fill this gap in critical writings on Gide by discussing *Si le grain ne meurt* from the perspectives of both literary history and textual analysis.

One of the principal reasons for the critical neglect of this work may well be the relative disrespect which most admittedly autobiographical first-person narratives have suffered over the years. Too often the notion has existed that there is no "art" to autobiography; for a writer who speaks of himself does so spontaneously, without invention, and thus, in more than one respect, "artlessly". The second purpose of our study is to illustrate, through the example of Gide's *Si le grain ne meurt*, that autobiography is indeed an art, a special literary genre with its own history, problems, and criteria for success.

The first chapter deals at some length with the question of autobiography as a literary genre. After examining André Gide's particular preoccupation with genre-classification, it surveys the genres related to autobiography (biography, memoirs, diaries, letters, autobiographical fiction, and even history and the novel) with a view to clarifying the rapport of the author of *Si le grain ne meurt* with each genre. This section

1

stresses the relative merits and handicaps of autobiography among the genres. Since originally writing this chapter, I have been led to redirect my emphasis. I had undertaken my research on what was — for scholars in the field of French literature at least — relatively virgin territory. As I was completing my manuscript, however, part of my task was prefigured in the publication of Philippe Lejeune's excellent study, *L'Autobiographie en France*. I was, of course, a little dismayed that M. Lejeune's fine bibliography necessarily duplicated my own and diminished its importance. At the same time, I was delighted to find myself less alone in my stand for the independence of autobiography as a literary genre and in my admiration for some outstanding examples in French literature. Furthermore, as M. Lejeune himself points out, the subject has still only just been grazed: a full history of the genre in France is yet to be written, and M. Lejeune's own useful definition of the genre is probably not the final word. It is, then, thanks to M. Lejeune that I have been able to abridge my original chapter and add new material. In my revisions, I have tried not to repeat unduly the ideas which he and I share; but if I do sometimes err in that direction, I hope that I will be forgiven by at least those readers who are not yet familiar with his work, and by those who sympathize with our mutual desire to propagandize in favour of this worthy literary genre.[1]

The second chapter traces the complex life-history of *Si le grain ne meurt* from conception, through gestation and birth, to its first few months in the public eye. Although the number of editions which Gide's autobiography underwent before general commercial release is exceptional by any standards, a study of its genesis and the early critical reaction is useful in shedding light on the problems that any autobiographer can experience.

Chapter III examines some of the structural and stylistic aspects of the text which are either typical of autobiography or characteristic of Gide's technique in this particular work. It

1. Stephen A. Shapiro reminds us that Wellek and Warren in their important *Theory of Literature* (originally published in 1942) were still reluctant to accept autobiography as a literary genre. Mr. Shapiro's valuable essay is significantly entitled "The Dark Continent of Literature: Autobiography", *Comparative Literature Studies* v (December 1968): 421-54.

As for M. Lejeune, he is evidently intent on refining his theories still further. See his more recent article, "Le Pacte autobiographique", *Poétique*, no. 14 (1973), pp. 137-62. M. Lejeune has also recently published two studies of particular relevance to *Si le grain ne meurt*: "Gide et l'autobiographie", in *André Gide*, 4 (Paris, 1974), and *Exercices d'ambiguité: Lectures de "Si le grain ne meurt" d'André Gide* (Paris, 1974).

deals with his use of foreshadowing, the peculiarities of verb tenses in the narration of an autobiography, the extent to which he varies his narrative techniques, and the role of lyricism, rhetoric, and irony in the work.

The famous Gidean "sincerity" is, once again, discussed in Chapter IV, where factual discrepancies, inconsistencies, contradictions, omissions, and misrepresentations are examined under the general title of "The Truth of an Autobiography". The solution proposed after an appraisal of Gide's "truthfulness" is applicable to other autobiographies.

Chapter V explores the idea that a well-written autobiography must inevitably resemble a novel in both content and structure. More precisely, it points out some of the novels that *Si le grain ne meurt* might call to mind, and attempts to show why.

The Conclusion optimistically hopes for a shift in emphasis in further studies of *Si le grain ne meurt*.

Finally, two appendices complete the volume. The genealogical tables of Appendix A are meant simply to help the reader identify Gide's family more rapidly on meeting them in the text, although at the same time they serve to link the autobiography to the "family" novels of the *grands bourgeois* of the 1920s. The notes on the manuscript in Appendix B are the first step towards a much-needed critical edition of *Si le grain ne meurt*.

I am grateful to Madame Catherine Gide and the Gide Committee for allowing me to consult the manuscript of *Si le grain ne meurt* at the Bibliothèque Jacques Doucet, and to the Canada Council for their tangible support during my sabbatical year of research. In various ways, Messrs. François Chapon and Romuald Szramkiewicz, and my colleagues, Professors Jacques Cotnam, Andrew Oliver, Réjean Robidoux, William Rogers, and Catherine Grisé have been invaluable in assisting me in the present study. To the last named I am additionally indebted for her wifely patience and encouragement.

The book has been published with the help of a grant from the Humanities Research Council of Canada, using funds provided by the Canada Council.

C.D.E.T.
Victoria College
University of Toronto

1

The
Genre
of Autobiography

NO FRENCH author of the twentieth century seems to have been more conscious of the question of literary genre than André Gide. Not only was he creatively active in virtually all the recognizable genres of his period — novel, poetry, theatre, essays, literary criticism, travel narratives, even libretti—he was also responsible for reinvigorating or redefining others: the imaginary interview, the diary, the *récit*, and the *sotie*, for instance. The fact that Gide's own commitment to distinctions between *récit*, *sotie*, and *roman* appears to have come about relatively late in his career and waned several years before his death has not lessened its importance in Gide studies, anxious as his critics are to grasp at any solid guidelines which their elusive subject might offer.[1] The result has been that for the purposes of university study — or even cocktail chit-chat — students and *aficionados* have smugly acknowledged that *Les Faux-monnayeurs* is Gide's only *true* novel ("in the Gidean sense, of course"). Three other works

---

1. For an example of the sort of lively discussion this subject has aroused, see the debate between Campbell Nairne and George Painter in three issues of *The Listener*, in 1948. After pointing out that Gide made his reclassification of his prose fiction only around 1914 in the cancelled preface to *Les Caves du Vatican*, Mr. Painter concludes that: "Gide himself since 1946 seems to have dropped his rather forced distinction. The list of works in *Thésée*, for instance, or the new edition of *Paludes* is unclassified. No doubt he feels the idea has by now registered — or perhaps he is tired of it." "The Novels of André Gide", *The Listener*, October 28, 1948, p. 649.

of fiction with a comic intention and unevenly reminiscent of some late-medieval dramatic spoofs are *soties;* so much for *Paludes, Le Prométhée mal enchaîné,* and *Les Caves du Vatican.* And as for the other fictional works, if narrated in the first person and dealing with a central moral dilemma handled with brevity and restraint, they qualify nicely as *récits.* No one would seem ready to argue, therefore, about the pedigree of *L'Immoraliste, La Porte étroite, Isabelle, La Symphonie pastorale, L'Ecole des femmes, Robert,* or *Geneviève*—even though some of these slipped into print before Gide had arrived at his neat genre formula, and have over the years shamelessly flaunted the label "roman" on their title pages.[2] As Gide himself allowed,[3] these works may be just as ironical as *soties*; but with the exception of certain pages of *Isabelle*, comic they are not.

As clear and acceptable as the *roman-récit-sotie* distinction may appear to most people today, the same is not true of all Gide's genre labels. Certain problems became particularly clear in 1958 at the time of publication of the Pléiade edition of Gide's *Romans; Récits et Soties; Oeuvres lyriques.* What, for instance, is a "traité", a term that the author had used within his own lifetime to classify six short and relatively early works? Although decidedly a didactic genre, the Gidean *traité* bears little resemblance to Descartes's work on the "passions". Far from being discursive essays, four of Gide's *traités—Le Traité du Narcisse, La Tentative amoureuse, El Hadj,* and *Le Retour de l'enfant prodigue*— are narrative in form, while *Philoctète* and *Bethsabé* appear to be short plays. These last two works are omitted from the Pléiade edition, the editors having, one assumes, agreed to group only the four narrative *traités* with the two volumes of *Nourritures* under the general heading of "Oeuvres lyriques". The editors of this highly respected series thereby succeeded in casting permanent scholarly doubt on a formerly unquestioned genre-grouping.

These same editors may well have had trouble classifying *Les Cahiers d'André Walter,* for they quite arbitrarily omitted it from their edition. On the basis of its lyricism and its narrative structure, *Les Cahiers d'André Walter* would seem to be every bit

---

2. *L'Immoraliste* and *La Porte étroite* in their various Mercure de France editions, including Le Livre de poche.
3. "Récits et Soties, je n'écrivis jusqu'à présent que des livres ironiques—ou critiques si l'on préfère, dont sans doute voici le dernier." Discarded preface to *Les Caves du Vatican* quoted by Gide in his *Journal*, le 30 juin 1914, p. 428. Unless otherwise indicated, all references to Gide's works give the pagination of the three-volume Pléiade edition.

as worthy of admission as *Thésée*, which *is* present. *Thésée*'s lyricism, which is most apparent in its oft-quoted final pages, may have been its qualifying element; but it is more likely that the editors classified it as a *récit* (as Gide himself had indicated). Nevertheless, *Thésée*'s classical setting and occasionally ribald tone seem slightly out of place alongside the contemporary, bourgeois, and serious *Immoraliste* and *Porte étroite*. Could *Thésée* not be posthumously called a *sotie*? On the other hand, in plot, setting, and tone, *Les Cahiers d'André Walter* bears strong enough resemblances to *La Porte étroite* to be unquestionably a *récit*. In spite of some relatively careful genre definitions and classifications in his lifetime, then, Gide still left room for further hesitation and debate on the part of his critics.

As an extreme example of an unresolved genre-classification, one need only look at *Le Voyage d'Urien*, which Gide did not label, and which remains eligible for a variety of categories. In structure, its narrative in three parts with *prélude* and *envoi* resembles the framed narrative triptych used by the author in his *traités, Le Traité du Narcisse* and *La Tentative amoureuse*. Furthermore, its content is didactic enough that it is surprising Gide did not apply to *Urien* the same sort of subtitle that he used for the original edition of *Paludes: Le Traité de la contingence*. On the other hand, its highly lyrical prose and its obvious parallels with Rimbaud's "Le Bateau ivre" tempt one to call it a *poème en prose*; its first-person narration, its brevity, and its didacticism qualify it as a *récit*; and the myth-and-symbol critics might very well see a modern *allégorie* in these pilgrims who set out at dawn to meet such symbols of temptation as sensuous women, exotic fruit, perfumes, and tepid baths. Mallarmé feared from the title that Gide might have perpetrated a literal travel account until he learned how improbable were the voyagers' misadventures. As improbable, we might add, and as pregnant with meaning as those of a Candide or Zadig in a *conte philosophique*. But finally, can *Le Voyage d'Urien* be anything but first and foremost a symbolist *roman* which was going to align its author with Maeterlinck and Mallarmé as the triumvirate of symbolist writers?[4] One wishes that the author of *Urien* had himself resolved the problem. Since he did not, *Le Voyage d'Urien* serves to underline how difficult it is to classify Gide's works precisely.

---

4. In the period of *André Walter*, Gide had said: "Donc, Mallarmé pour la poésie, Maeterlinck pour le drame—et, [...] j'ajoute Moi pour le roman." Lettre d'André Gide à Paul Valéry, le 26 janvier 1891, *Correspondance André Gide-Paul Valéry, 1890-1942* (Paris, 1955), p. 46.

And woe to the critic who sees the the task as simple!

Of all Gide's works, *Si le grain ne meurt* would at first glance seem to offer the least problem in regard to the identification of its genre. It narrates, in a more or less orderly fashion, the first twenty-five and a half years in André Gide's life—from his birth on November 22, 1869, until his engagement to his cousin, Madeleine Rondeaux, in the summer of 1895. The work has been sometimes published with the subtitle "Souvenirs d'enfance et de jeunesse", and Gide refers to it himself as his "Mémoires" or "Souvenirs". He continued, in fact, to use the word "Mémoires" long after choosing the final title on January 11, 1917.[5] Never does he use the word autobiography. *Si le grain ne meurt* is, therefore, clearly a book of memoirs — the recollections of André Gide.

But we have already seen that Gide's application of a generic name to a work should not necessarily close the critical debate on its ultimate classification. In the pigeon-holing of *Si le grain ne meurt,* as elsewhere, we must ask: Can we trust Gide? Some of his critics would seem to think so. Justin O'Brien, for instance, refers to *Si le grain ne meurt* as Gide's memoirs.[6] Charles Du Bos, however, allows that the longer first part is "Mémoires", whereas the shorter, and (according to Du Bos) more insidious, second part is autobiography. In his important study, the first detailed analysis of *Si le grain ne meurt*, Du Bos sums up his impressions as follows: "La Première Partie ressortit à l'ordre du mémorialiste — d'un mémorialiste tout ensemble musard, sautillant, et pourtant infiniment concerté; la Deuxième Partie en revanche est le récit à bride abattue, indivisible, infaillible en son mouvement, d'une stridente et jubilante obsession."[7] Du Bos's personal definitions appear to have banned sexual allusions from memoirs while admitting them to autobiography. When he sees traces of autobiography in the earlier part, too, he is referring to Gide's discussion of his sexual practices. In general, though, he sees Gide's work as hybrid, with the differences evident in the tone and tempo of the two parts. Since the time of Du Bos, but not necessarily because of him, most critics have called *Si le grain ne meurt* an autobiography. Some,

---

5. See, for instance, the *Journal, 1889-1939*, pp. 547, 551-2, 556, 572, 584, 585, 612, 614, 615, 617, 618, 620, 622, 632, 634, 643, 644, 659, 685, 687, 690, and 695; or in the text of *Si le grain ne meurt* itself, pp. 369, 434, 487, 492, 530, 547.
6. Justin O'Brien, *Portrait of André Gide* (London, 1953), pp. 259, 262.
7. Charles Du Bos, *Le Dialogue avec André Gide* (Paris, 1929), p. 268.

however, have complicated the issue. George Painter, for instance, only a page after he has called the work an autobiography, states: *"If It Die* is a confession."[8] Enid Starkie rather ambiguously says: "It ranks amongst the great autobiographies of the world, though it is nearer in form to confessions."[9] And quite recently, Jean Delay returned unequivocally to the term "Mémoires".[10]

Until late 1971, the most satisfying guide to determining the genre of a suspected autobiography was the definition (and valuable related research) of Roy Pascal in his *Design and Truth in Autobiography*. Pascal insisted the autobiographer give an account "which involves the reconstruction of the movement of a life, or part of a life, in the actual circumstances in which it was lived."[11] He emphasized the fact that an autobiography's centre of interest must be the narrator's self rather than the outside world, granting that the outside world must indeed appear in the work in its double role as both backdrop to and partner with the narrator's actions and the evolution of his personality. Memoirs, on the other hand, downplay or even ignore the notion of the narrator's evolving personality, stressing instead events and people external to him.

This distinction alone would appear to satisfy us that *Si le grain ne meurt* is an autobiography rather than a volume of memoirs; for Gide succeeds in tracing clearly the development of a constrained, retiring child into a well-read, curious, and creative young man of extraordinary psychological complexity. At almost all times the Gidean personality is the core of interest, and other people — whether in confining Normandy or in liberating Africa — serve as a background to or explanation for the crucial drama that the reader is witnessing. Gide's own understating of the purely literary aspects of his life in favour of psychological influences has made it almost irrelevant to the reader that his career was finally that of a man of letters. He states, in fact, that he could easily have been a biologist or a musician instead, and we learn almost as much about his youthful botanizing and piano lessons as we do about his early exposure to French composition and literature. We do not read

---

8. George D. Painter, *André Gide: A Critical Biography* (London, 1968), p. 79.
9. Enid Starkie, *André Gide* (Cambridge, 1953), p. 38.
10. Jean Delay, "Gide ou l'expérience de soi", in *Cahiers André Gide*, 3 (Paris, 1972), p. 82.
11. Roy Pascal, *Design and Truth in Autobiography* (London, 1960), p. 5.

this work for the same reason that we read the memoirs of, for instance, Charles de Gaulle or even André Maurois. Here, the historical events are absent; the literary name-dropping is minimal. The emphasis is personal and sometimes exceedingly intimate. We cannot help realizing that we are dealing with the autobiography of an exceptionally talented and fascinating man rather than with the memoirs of an epoch-making public figure. As we have seen, reaching this conclusion has not always been so simple. It has been only within the past fifteen years or so that theoreticians on autobiographical writings have attempted to define their terms more clearly.[12] Until then, and sometimes even now, the term autobiography could carelessly refer not only to memoirs or to autobiography as we define it here, but also to confessions, diaries, letters, and autobiographical novels.

With the publication in 1971 of Philippe Lejeune's study on French autobiography, certain dangling uncertainties about definition seem at last to have been resolved. Roy Pascal had, for instance, allowed for lyric poetry to be classified as autobiography, citing Wordsworth's *Prelude* as the earliest English masterpiece — a British parallel to Rousseau and Goethe. By Pascal's loose definition, literally hundreds of volumes of French poetry would have to be admitted to the genre, including such justly famous but factually spurious works as Lamartine's *Méditations* and Hugo's *Contemplations* — doctored dates of composition and all. Lejeune was quick to outlaw poetry from the genre. His definition reads as follows: "Nous appelons autobiographie le récit rétrospectif en prose que quelqu'un fait de sa propre existence quand il met l'accent principal sur l'histoire de sa personnalité."[13] Lejeune's definition also implicitly bans from the genre diaries and letters (because they are not retrospective narratives) and — like Roy Pascal — memoirs (because their principal perspective is other than the story of the narrator's evolving personality). All fiction, of course — including autobiographical fiction — is excluded. Although Lejeune does not mention the term, his definition also bans "confessions", a word which in general twentieth-century usage has come to mean a racy sub-literary form of writing whose avowals of true revelations are mere pretexts for exhibitionistic fabrications destined to sell well on the newsstand. A sad destiny for a

---

12. See the list of works on autobiography in the Bibliography.
13. Philippe Lejeune, *L'Autobiographie en France* (Paris, 1971), p. 14.

9

word which when used by Saint Augustine or Jean-Jacques Rousseau assumed unquestionable stature![14]

Lejeune's definition would seem to be unexceptionable for most scholars. However, his further exposition on the subject reveals that his application of it is more rigid than the definition at first suggests. He admits himself that not all will agree with his requirement that to be accredited as a full-fledged autobiography a work must contain a substantial amount of childhood data and reminiscences.[15] Equally controversial is his stricture that an account of a relatively short isolated portion of a life (such as Stendhal's *Souvenirs d'égotisme*) should be discredited as a valid example of autobiography. Lejeune stringently requires as well that each acceptable autobiography contain some statement or pact of the author's intention of telling the true story of his life. This requirement would have disqualified Simone de Beauvoir's *Mémoires d'une jeune fille rangée* had she not remedied the situation in the prologue to *La Force de l'âge*.

All this aside, Lejeune's study brings order to our subject and aids us immeasurably in reinforcing our insistence on the legitimate status of *Si le grain ne meurt* as an autobiography.

What kind of man or woman will write a book about himself? Is he vain? The opinion seems to be that while he may indeed be egotistical, he is more often curious—about the kind of person he really is, and how he came to be that way. Writing, then, becomes a self-exploratory function. The autobiographer may be taking pleasure in expressing himself about himself, or, on the contrary, may be attempting to reconcile his own conscience. He may have a mission such as to make people believe that the personality with which he confronts the world is authentic; or else (as in the case of Rousseau) that he was not as

14. That is not to say that it is impossible to envisage a creditable volume of serious confessions in the twentieth century; George Painter and Enid Starkie, in the passages referred to previously, were by no means using "confessions" pejoratively. It is just that the examples are so rare! A curious contemporary example of the confessional mode used in fiction is Albert Camus's *La Chute*, where ironically enough the protagonist, Jean-Baptiste Clamence, states: "D'ailleurs je n'aime plus que les confessions, et les auteurs de confession écrivent surtout pour ne pas se confesser, pour ne rien dire de ce qu'ils savent. Quand ils prétendent passer aux aveux c'est le moment de se méfier, on va maquiller le cadavre." *La Chute* (Paris, 1956), pp. 140-1. See also Peter M. Axthelm, *The Modern Confessional Novel* (New Haven, 1967).

15. Lejeune hastens to add that not all childhood reminiscences are necessarily autobiographies. He eliminates Maurice Genevoix's *Au Cadran de mon clocher*, Sacha Guitry's *Si j'ai bonne mémoire*, and Albert Cohen's *Le Livre de ma mère* from the genre. Lejeune, *L'Autobiographie en France*, p. 21.

the world saw him. Rousseau wrote to prove his uniqueness. Montaigne, who is an ancestor of all autobiographers without actually participating in the genre as we describe it here, wrote to show how representative of all men *he* was. Some seemingly less ambitious writers — like Sartre — write of themselves as merely representative of a generation.[16] Others write to convince us (sometimes modestly or indirectly) of a personal doctrine. In all cases, the successful autobiographer is someone who clearly recognizes that his self of today is different from, yet totally indebted to, his self of yesterday, and may very well be different again tomorrow. Consciously or unconsciously, at the time of writing, it is for posterity that he is recording his two equally impermanent selves — the present and the past. And it will be primarily these selves *as he records them* which posterity will remember. Finally, it is not unsafe to say that virtually everyone who writes about himself believes there is a lesson to be learned from his recorded example. Such is unquestionably the case in the composition of *Si le grain ne meurt.*

It might be helpful at this point to consider why André Gide might have been motivated to use autobiography rather than other possible means to relate the story of his life with its intrinsic message. It will be seen that some genres were generally unsuited to his creative propensities, but that even those genres most closely related to autobiography—and to his native talents — would have been inadequate for the directness of expression to which he aspired.

One can list the possible genres in a descending order representing the decreasing importance attributed either explicitly or implicitly to factual accuracy in each undertaking: (1) History, (2) Biography, (3) Memoirs, (4) Diaries and Letters, (5) Autobiography, (6) Autobiographical Fiction, (7) Fiction.[17]

---

16. Before the publication of *Les Mots* (1964), Sartre spoke of his intention to write his autobiography in *The Listener,* June 6, 1957.

17. For clarification of the genre scheme, it is useful to turn to the example of George Sand. The lady is only of peripheral interest to HISTORY; however, *Lélia,* a fine volume of BIOGRAPHY, has been written about her by André Maurois. She wrote a DIARY and copious LETTERS which are being methodically edited in many volumes by Georges Lubin. Her *Histoire de ma vie* tells exactly what its title promises; and because of its point of view, we prefer to classify it as AUTOBIOGRAPHY rather than MEMOIRS. She also wrote much AUTOBIOGRAPHICAL FICTION, one novel of which was not coincidentally called *Lélia.* All of these works cover some of the same material from their author's busy life and are profitably explored together in genre studies. In our final category, FICTION, George Sand wrote such non-autobiographical novels as *François le Champi,* which, unlike her autobiographical fiction, was

11

The first genre is the remotest from autobiography, and is quite clearly alien to Gide's nature, intentions, and situation. He often spoke of his lack of interest in reading history, and in spite of the factual data that appear in the early chapters of *Si le grain ne meurt,* it is difficult to imagine two treatments of identical material more dissimilar than his and the fulsomely detailed family history written by his cousin by marriage, Pierre Le Verdier.[18] Furthermore, a fully documented family history is hardly a logical project for the man who uttered the now apparently immortal, "Familles, je vous hais." And it would not be with impunity that a writer would use sacred family lore as a pretext for displaying the evolution of his own rather profane individuality. In passing, it is interesting to note that history, which the manuals of literary history assure us was a full-fledged literary genre in the nineteenth century, seems to have fallen outside the realm of literature in the twentieth. Are we to assume that Gide's indifference to history was only the natural reaction of a literary man who recognized earlier than most that it was wrongly classified?

Only the remaining six genres can be considered "literary", and these not all of the time. A well-researched modern biography, with no special literary pretensions, more and more in outward appearance approaches *history* as a mode of writing,

---

suitable reading even for children—like the protagonist of *A la recherche du temps perdu.*

However, in case we begin to feel smug about our neat genre-classification, all we need do is remind ourselves that not all autobiographical novels are written in the first person, as we see in some works of Colette. Nor for that matter are all first-person novels necessarily autobiographical. The *Journal d'un curé de campagne* of Bernanos bears witness to this. To add to the confusion, we find E. K. Brown telling us in *Rhythm in the Novel* (p. 33) that Flaubert himself described the epitome of all novels, *Madame Bovary,* as a "biography". Furthermore, Flaubert's famous "Madame Bovary, c'est moi" inevitably encourages an examination of this work as autobiographical fiction. We read a short, fulsome biography of the philosopher-critic Alain and find it signed by the author himself, thus making it a delightfully ironical autobiography—*La Table Ronde,* no. 89 (mai 1955), pp. 77-82. To complicate matters further, Anatole France is often quoted from his preface to *La Vie Littéraire* as saying that "Tout roman, à le bien prendre, est une autobiographie," and Cocteau says that *every*thing we write is a self-portrait—"Lettre-préface" for the *Festgabe für Fritz Neubert,* p. 9. Alain Girard includes all the arts when he says: "Toute construction esthétique est toujours plus ou moins autobiographique"—"Le *Journal* dans l'oeuvre de Gide", in *Entretiens sur André Gide* (La Haye, 1967), p. 191.

18. Pierre Le Verdier, *Une famille de haute bourgeoisie rouennaise: Histoire de la famille Rondeaux* (Rouen, 1928).

thus also abandoning its right to classification as "literature". The severe criticism of André Maurois's early and highly fictionalized *Ariel ou la Vie de Shelley* convinced many subsequent biographers (and Maurois himself) that this genre must depend heavily on rigid documentation for its authority, sometimes at the expense of stylistic artistry. There is no place for imaginary scenes or re-created dialogues and monologues outside of *biographie romancée* (which in its most blatant incarnation falls in the final category of our list). The valuable biographer must resign himself to fettering his imagination.

Some authors have found fascinating kindred spirits whose biographies have served as a framework for some of their own preoccupations. We have, accordingly, Chateaubriand's *Vie de Rancé,* Mauriac's *Vie de Jésus,* and even Sartre's study of Flaubert. But in Gide's case, the essay or lecture format and regular journal jottings proved satisfactory as a means for discussion of such figures as Dostoievsky, Goethe, Montaigne, and Stendhal, whose ideas and works were, after all, more akin to him than their lives.[19] His own specialness, as we shall see, could not emerge satisfactorily in the biography of someone else. Certainly Gertrude Stein's experimental playfulness in using the guise of writing the biography of someone else (in the first person yet) while actually writing her *own* story (*The Autobiography of Alice B. Toklas*) could well have appealed to the author of *Les Caves du Vatican*; however, the story that Gide had to tell was far too serious for these or other contrivances.

Gide would have found memoirs almost as unsuitable a means as history and biography for talking about himself. Memoirs, though most often written in the first person and founded on personal recollections (like autobiography), aim primarily to perpetuate factual information for future generations (like history and biography). Yet even here the rules are not watertight, since Caesar wrote his memoirs in the third person, and more than one memorialist has forsaken historical truth for gossipy chatter or self-vindication. But most memorialists are prominent public figures important enough to believe that their readers might be interested in the reasons for their success, or in the historical or private events which they have had the fortune or misfortune to observe closely. Their purpose in writing is less to explain a personality than to inform a public. Two cases in point are the memoirs of Charles de

19. There are, of course, examples of such writers as Oscar Wilde and Roger Martin du Gard whom Gide *knew,* and whose lives were more interesting or dearer to him than their works.

13

Gaulle and those of Winston Churchill, both of whom, while happening to add to our knowledge of their personalities, first and foremost treat of historical events and people other than themselves. The memorialist, then, has a fixed concrete purpose in mind and finds himself in the position of having the criteria for selecting the events of his memoirs preordained. While he may overstep these bounds—and sometimes with considerable success, as in the case of Chateaubriand, who shifts his position as *Les Mémoires d'outre-tombe* progress to write what is to a large extent an autobiography—most memorialists have chosen to stick to their single purpose. The most prevalent sort of memorialists seem to be statesmen, politicians, military figures, missionaries, and scientists.

To be a true memorialist, then, Gide would have had to undertake an account of his life with an emphasis on what impelled him to become a writer, or who helped him along the way. This was not the case, for Gide first conceived the idea of writing frankly of his life even before 1900: "Selon vous, je n'aurais 'pris que sur le tard cette détermination d'écrire mes mémoires.' Quelques amis communs pourront vous certifier que cette détermination avec toutes ses conséquences fut prise dès avant 1900; et non seulement la détermination de les écrire, mais bien aussi celle de les publier de mon vivant. Et de même pour *Corydon*."[20] At no more than thirty years of age, and with virtually no commercial literary success behind him, Gide was hardly at a point in his career when he could be motivated to write like our complacent and prestigious memorialists.

It could even be argued that when he actually began to write *Si le grain ne meurt* early in 1916, he was still not famous enough to be encouraged to write memoirs for an impatient following. His first commercial success had occurred only seven years earlier with *La Porte étroite*, and he would have to wait almost another three years before the post-war youth would find a timely message in *Les Nourritures terrestres* of 1897, or the Dadaïstes would see some anti-literary tendencies in the fun of *Les Caves du Vatican* (1914). Although forty-six years old in 1916, Gide was by no means the celebrity that he would be ten years later at the time of the general circulation of *Si le grain ne meurt*, or, of course, twenty years later at the time of his trip to Russia, or thirty years later on the threshold of a Nobel Prize.

Moreover, the very material which Gide was later to regret

20. From a letter dated January 1928 to François Porché (author of *L'Amour qui n'ose pas dire son nom*) published in Gide's *Oeuvres complètes*, 15 vols. (Paris, 1932-9), IX: 323.

having omitted from *Si le grain ne meurt* was a discussion of the literary sources that contributed to his artistic inspiration: "Je voudrais écrire, ne fût-ce que par reconnaissance, l'éloge des oeuvres qui m'ont appris à me connaître, qui m'ont formé. Le grand défaut de *Si le grain ne meurt*: je n'y dis point quels furent mes initiateurs. Il y aurait là matière à un autre livre, et sur un plan tout différent. Mais c'est il y a quinze ans qu'il aurait été bon de l'écrire."[21] Gide himself recognized that the book on the formation of "André Gide — author" would have been a different work from *Si le grain ne meurt*. It would have been more in keeping with what readers expect from memoirs of famous authors, and would probably have included an appraisal of the significance of his role in the literary world, his influence on French and international literary movements, the names of younger writers whom he encouraged, and so on. Such a work could only have been written when his reputation was finally secure.

As for diaries and letters, Gide was already an old hand at them both, but the special attributes of these allied genres did not fully suit his purposes. By writing his *Journal* from day to day, Gide had recognized that all subjects are open to diarists. Philosophical and sentimental recollections are as valid as accounts of dinner parties — and in Gide's hands, usually more fruitful. But Gide doubtless also knew that the random recollections of the diarist are no substitute for the sequential, evolving narrative structure that he needed for his desired effect.

Each new published volume of Gide's correspondence proves further that he is one of the best practitioners of the epistolary art in French literary history.[22] He is doubtless also one of the last, for letters have become much less common in the age of the telephone. The few published correspondences of the literary generations since Gide's time serve more often as peripheral biographical documents than as a means of reinstating the letter as a major genre, which it was in the days of Madame de Sévigné. Gide's private correspondence was, we are to assume, not being written with publication explicitly in mind. Moreover, his now-published letters naturally tended to di-

---

21. *Journal*, le 21 août 1940, p. 50.
22. André Gide's correspondence with —among others— Arnold Bennett, Paul Claudel, Jean Cocteau, Charles Du Bos, Edmund Gosse, Francis Jammes, Roger Martin du Gard, François Mauriac, Marcel Proust, Rainer Maria Rilke, André Rouveyre, André Suarès, and Paul Valéry has already been published. Editions of Gide's correspondence with Mme Paul Gide, Pierre Louÿs, Marcel Drouin, Jean Schlumberger, Dorothy Bussy, and Pierre de Massot are now in preparation.

vulge his current actions and thoughts rather than describe an increasingly distant childhood. For these reasons, and since the genre suffers from the same fragmentary effect one finds in a diary, it would not do at all. Nor would an open letter to yet another Nathanaël. By its very tradition as a tool for heavy-handed propaganda, the open letter often dissuades as many readers as it convinces. Besides, isn't any piece of published writing aimed at a particular audience in some sense an open letter? Gide could never have considered so unsubtle a means as this to tell his story.

Leaving aside for the moment autobiography itself, we now reach autobiographical fiction and fiction in our list. The difference between the two is merely that while neither genre has any inherent obligation to present factual information, the former will contain recognizable events from the author's life—usually expressed in the first person. Aside from this, both modes allow for a novelist's infinite inventiveness. Now Gide had already reproduced two of the most important episodes of his life-story in his *récits*, *L'Immoraliste* and *La Porte étroite*. The crucial trips to North Africa in the 1890s had in a modified form furnished the very structure of the former, while the traumatic childhood discovery on the rue de Lecat had provided the basic pretext for the love plot in the latter. But told by narrators named Michel and Jérôme, who were not meant to be totally true reflections of either the character or the natural style of André Gide, any personal message he wanted to convey had become fragmented and veiled. Indeed, the few readers who encountered *L'Immoraliste* when it was first published almost consistently missed its homosexual aspects.

As for the kind of fiction that is more clearly removed from the author's personal experiences, the author of the very inventive *Caves du Vatican* had further developments in mind which had nothing to do with an autobiographical project. Paradoxically, Gide discovered while composing *Si le grain ne meurt* that the novel form could perhaps have served his purposes better. "Les Mémoires," says Gide, "ne sont jamais qu'à demi sincères, si grand que soit le souci de vérité: tout est toujours plus compliqué qu'on ne le dit. Peut-être même approche-t-on de plus près la vérité dans le roman." [23] Gide is here referring to how *unnatural* it is to delve beyond a certain point in intimate revelations—and this in a genre which demands naturalness at all costs. He is also concerned over his own urge to simplify a

23. *Si le grain ne meurt*, p. 547n.

subject the complexity of which he recognizes only too well. Perhaps he is alluding indirectly as well to certain restrictions imposed by the technique of first-person narration. Though *seeming* to know all about his subject (himself), the narrator in fact does not, and is hampered in remedying this by limitations in potential points of view. When an autobiographer strays from his own range of knowledge, he must clearly document his sources, whereas the hero of a novel may be viewed from the outside by a variety of characters easily manipulated by the author. As Roy Pascal puts it: "The autobiographer can neither get inside other people nor outside himself."[24] In the *Journal des Faux-monnayeurs*, Gide adds further: "Je fus amené [. . .] à penser que l'intimité, la pénétration, l'investigation psychologique peut, à certains égards, être poussée plus avant dans le 'roman' que même dans les 'confessions'. L'on est parfois gêné dans celles-ci par le 'je'; il y a certaines complexités que l'on ne peut chercher à démêler, à étaler sans apparence de complaisance."[25] A novelist has no important vested interests in or obligations to his imaginary characters and can analyse and invent or even experiment with them to his heart's content; but for a variety of reasons—timidity, repugnance, modesty—the autobiographer will not treat *himself* with the same brutality, and will finally have written what is in part fictitious. In the case of Gide, Marguerite Yourcenar has stated, immediately after finding a good deal of Gide's life in his novel *Les Faux-monnayeurs*: "Il y a des moments [dans *Si le grain ne meurt*] où Gide va très loin dans l'expression de soi; il y a des moments, surtout dans les récits de l'enfance, où il reste un peu sur le seuil de lui-même, comme s'il s'agissait d'un enfant quelconque dont il racontait l'histoire. . . ."[26] She goes on to speak of "certains 'Souvenirs' un peu désultoires" and "cette superficialité" before casting doubt on the "vérité totale" of Gide's account of even the sexual experiences. It is not surprising that a novelist like Yourcenar should sense the fiction-writer's normal tendency to create, even when limited in scope by the autobiographical dictum of *re*-creation of character and event.

24. Pascal, *Design and Truth,* p. 177.
25. *Journal des Faux-monnayeurs,* p. 27. I am grateful to Professor Réjean Robidoux for reminding me of the importance of this passage. Other autobiographers, incidentally, share Gide's frustration with the level of sincerity attainable in the autobiography. See François Mauriac's *Commencements d'une vie*, p. xv, for this author's stand in favour of the novel.
26. Marguerite Yourcenar, "André Gide Revisited", in *Cahiers André Gide*, 3 (Paris, 1972), p. 36.

In our representation of decreasing relative concern for factuality among the related genres, we have placed autobiography between diaries and autobiographical fiction. This suggests that an autobiographer is less committed to the kind of veracity which is obligatory for a memorialist and which usually comes naturally to a diarist. *Less* committed, yes, but not *un*committed. Readers seem to accept, for instance, an autobiographer's occasional verbatim reconstruction of a dialogue or monologue that occurred decades earlier, but at the same time they demand that every writer who calls his work an autobiography have a firm respect for truth. This truth is one of self, of self-representation, if you wish. It is this alone which counts. We are able, indeed almost always *obliged*, to excuse inconsistencies in factual detail in an autobiography. As Georg Misch points out, "Almost every autobiography can be shown to be deficient in detailed accuracy."[27] Some factual inconsistencies are due to a poor memory, others to faulty informants. Sometimes the perceptiveness or judgement of the autobiographer himself will have been at fault. But even conscious distortions of the truth can be excusable in autobiography. Georges Gusdorf rejects the importance of hunting for the inaccuracies in Chateaubriand's *Mémoires d'outre-tombe*, observing that: "Fiction ou imposture, la valeur d'art est réelle; une *vérité* s'atteste par delà les truquages d'itinéraire et de chronologie, *vérité* de l'homme, images de soi et du monde, rêves de l'homme de génie, qui se réalise dans l'irréel, pour son propre enchantement et celui de ses lecteurs."[28] Historical truth in autobiography, then, is less important than a kind of personal truth. And as Roy Pascal suggests, the kind of romanticizing that we find in, say, Ernest Renan's account of his early life, provided it does not go too far, becomes merely a stylistic attribute of the work.[29]

What does the reader glean from autobiographies? From their content, he may learn more about mankind, how he thinks, behaves, and evolves; he may gain insight into the society of a certain period in history; he may become indoctrinated with a new philosophical, religious, or ethical doctrine, or may become repelled by the same; he may share in a love of life, or enjoy the catharsis of being moved by sorrow; he may be

27. Georg Misch, *A History of Autobiography in Antiquity*, 2 vols. (London, 1950), I: 11.
28. Georges Gusdorf, "Conditions et limites de l'autobiographie", in *Festgabe für Fritz Neubert: Formen der Selbstdarstellung* (Berlin, 1956), p. 119. The italics are mine.
29. Pascal, *Design and Truth*, p. 68.

entertained by humorous events, or find escape from his normal existence in the glamorous or exotic lives of others. In short, he may be informed or entertained by *both* history *and* fiction, while also indulging the urge to discover intimate secrets, which autobiography so uniquely satisfies. And depending on the style of the work, he may have the added pleasure of contact with an aesthetically pleasing literary work. As a reader of the most important French autobiographies of the eighteenth and nineteenth centuries — those of Rousseau, Chateaubriand, Stendhal, and Renan—Gide must certainly have been well aware of the particular advantages of this genre.[30]

In order better to assess Gide's place in the history of the genre, it would be well to turn back briefly to its origins. To begin with, there is little dispute that the father of all modern autobiographical writing is St. Augustine, although Georg Misch, as early as 1907, managed to fill two bulky volumes of *A History of Autobiography in Antiquity* in which he allowed that there were already eight full-length autobiographies in a very strict sense of the term before the time of Augustine.[31] Critics and historians since Misch still date their studies from Augustine, however, and insist that autobiographical writing is a strictly Occidental phenomenon, efforts like Gandhi's being borrowings of the pattern.[32] It seemed that a world of Christian conscience was for a long time necessary for writers in the genre — writers who might be tempted, like Rousseau, to call their works "confessions". Philippe Lejeune lucidly explains how the seventeenth- and eighteenth-century memoir-writers paved the way for Rousseau's searching self-examination, written between 1762 and 1770.[33]

The term "autobiography" was apparently first used in Eng-

30. See the *Journal* index for references to *Les Confessions, Les Mémoires d'outre-tombe, La Vie de Henry Brulard,* and the *Souvenirs d'enfance et de jeunesse.*
31. Reference is made here to the 1950 translation of this work, which was originally published in German and included volumes on medieval autobiography. Also pertinent is Pierre Courcelle, *Les "Confessions" de Saint-Augustin dans la tradition littéraire, antécédents et postérité* (Paris, 1963).
32. Gusdorf, "Conditions et limites de l'autobiographie", p. 117.
33. The *Dictionnaire des lettres françaises,* "Le Dix-huitième Siècle" (Paris, 1960), discusses the genres of the period under the headings "Dictionnaires et encyclopédie, Philosophie, Eloquence, Souvenirs et mémoires, Historiens, Théâtre, Roman, Poètes, Pamphlétaires, Littérature épistolaire", pp. 4-18. Jean-Jacques Rousseau's *Confessions* are treated with a respect that ignores their eighteenth-century reception.

land, where it appeared in print for the first time in 1809 when Robert Southey made use of it in a *Quarterly Review* article.[34] The *Dictionnaire historique de la langue française* (1894) lists as its first and only example of usage, "Les autobiographies sont souvent mensongères", from the *Dictionnaire de L'Académie* of 1878 — an entry which is significant for more than just its late-nineteenth-century date. The more recent *Dictionnaire Robert* indicates that "autobiographie" existed as early as 1842.

Roy Pascal insists on the years from 1782 (the publication of the First Part of Rousseau's *Confessions*) to 1831 (Goethe's *Dichtung und Wahrheit*) as being the decisive dates in the legitimization of autobiography as a conscious literary genre. He notes that in France, "Chateaubriand is only partly, Stendhal only just outside the limits of these dates."[35] Lejeune's "Répertoire pour servir à l'histoire de l'autobiographie en France" assembled in 1971 acknowledges the existence of no more than eighty full-fledged French autobiographers since Rousseau.[36] The highlights of the nineteenth century have already been mentioned, including (in note 17) the *Histoire de ma vie* of George Sand. The best of the twentieth century—besides *Si le grain ne meurt*—are probably the works of François Mauriac, Julien Green, Michel Leiris, Jean-Paul Sartre, Violette Leduc, Simone de Beauvoir, and André Gorz, all of which have been preceded (and influenced?) by Gide's general publication in 1926.

It would certainly appear that in both quantity and quality the genre has been at its richest during the past fifty years. Its progress has not yet halted; for confronted by the aesthetic experiments of the *nouveau roman*, general readers and literary critics alike are looking more and more to autobiography as a satisfying substitute for the values of story line, character study, and coherency which they used to find in the novel.[37] One can begin reading an autobiography with the assurance of finding a central figure who will tell you about his birth, his parents, his family life, his schooling, his religious training (or lack of it), his friends, his reading habits — and often his earliest sexual

---

34. See Jacques Voisine, "Naissance et évolution du terme littéraire 'autobiographie'", in *La Littérature comparée en Europe orientale, conférence de Budapest, 26-29 octobre 1962* (Budapest, 1963), pp. 278-86.

35. Pascal, *Design and Truth*, p. 50n.

36. See Lejeune, *L'Autobiographie en France*, pp. 106-37.

37. See the papers by Pierre de Boisdeffre and Jacques Borel on autobiography in *Positions et oppositions sur le roman contemporain: Actes du Colloque de Strasbourg* (Paris, 1971). Professor Phyllis Grosskurth expressed similar observations in a public lecture on autobiography at University College, University of Toronto, in early 1973.

experiences and first departure from home. All autobiographies seem to offer this information. But each one is different; the best can seem even original, unforgettably distinctive. Structure and style are a matter of the author's personal selection, of course; but generally speaking, each autobiographer will employ his artistic sense to choose a form that will harmonize with his view of himself, a view which will itself have been qualified by his intentions in writing the autobiography. Throughout this chapter, we have been referring too obliquely to the intentions of André Gide. It is time to be more explicit by examining the genesis of *Si le grain ne meurt*.

2

The Genesis of an Autobiography

FROM the letter to François Porché cited in the preceding chapter, we have seen that Gide had envisaged writing a story of his life even before 1900. According to Jean Delay's research, as early as 1894 Gide asked his mother for a "tableau chronologique" of his childhood. In 1897 at Alei ʾon he was already writing some fragments from a file of preparatory notes which he had assembled under the general title of *De me ipse et de aliis* [*sic*].[1]

It would seem that right from the first Gide's purpose was quite clear. It was certainly entirely so by the time he started writing. In October 1916, he refers indirectly to his true subject. He has been disheartened by rereading some of his early pages, and complains that he has not even reached his important material: "Et je n'y ai même pas abordé mon sujet, et l'on ne peut même encore entrevoir l'annonce, ni pressentir l'approche, de ce qui devait occuper tout le livre, de ce pourquoi j'écris. J'en suis à ne plus savoir si je dois continuer."[2] In January he hints at the controversial nature of his purpose: "Je n'écris pas ces Mémoires pour me défendre. Je n'ai point à me défendre, puisque je ne suis pas accusé. Je les écris avant d'être accusé. Je les écris pour qu'on m'accuse."[3] Still discouraged, he is more

---

1. See Jean Delay, *La Jeunesse d'André Gide*, 2 vols. (Paris, 1956-7), I: 9 and II: 388. The Catalogue of the Bibliothèque Nationale exhibition of 1970 refers to this inaccessible document as merely *De me ipse*. In either case, the grammatical error (*ipse* for *ipso*) remains.
2. *Journal,* le 13 octobre 1916, p. 572.
3. *Journal,* le 19 janvier 1917, p. 614.

specific about the essentially prefatory role of the recollections of childhood: "Je n'ai rien abordé, rien effleuré de ce qui me les fait écrire. Peut-être m'attardai-je à l'excès à ces bagatelles du vestibule."[4] His purpose during the composition of *Si le grain ne meurt* was, explicitly, to write a long account of an unspectacular childhood in which readers could find points of identification. Several true incidents of nervous hysteria or sexual precociousness would be in keeping with the traditional view of the artistic temperament, and would pave the way for the revelation of his homosexuality in the final part. The leisurely presentation of childhood would be necessary to prove that the homosexual adult had led a relatively happy and normal childhood; and the sexual games on the opening page would be a factor in unifying the two parts. Gide was using, then, a form of writing which he believed to be "Mémoires" to preach a lesson of tolerance for the homosexual, and his indoctrinating purpose would be subtly guiding details of his composition.

Gide's fullest explanation of his purpose in writing the work occurs in an eloquent letter to Sir Edmund Gosse, dated le 16 janvier 1927. He emphasizes a motivating sense of obligation behind it, an altruistic urge to give a precedent-setting example of frankness, to enlighten some and reassure others, to force public opinion to take account of a subject about which most people are ignorant or misinformed. Finally, he is anxious that he should be remembered correctly by posterity: "J'ai écrit ce livre parce qu je préfère être haï qu'aimé pour ce que je ne suis pas."[5] In this letter Gide did not differentiate between writing and publishing the work, a distinction he made more carefully in a "Projet de préface pour *Si le grain ne meurt*" which never did accompany any of the separate editions of the work. This preface covers largely the same arguments as the letter to Gosse, but it

4. *Journal,* le 21 janvier 1917, p. 615.
5. *The Correspondence of André Gide and Edmund Gosse, 1904-1928* (London, 1960), p. 190. An interesting variant of this letter was published by Gide in the *Nouvelle Revue Française,* juillet 1928, pp. 49-50. Peter C. Hoy discusses this letter in "From André Gide to Edmund Gosse", *American Notes and Queries*, n.s., ii (November 1963): 36-8. It is Hoy's opinion that Gide inserted in the N.R.F. version a short dialogue which served to publicize his determination in overcoming the opposition of his close friends who advised him against publication of *Si le grain ne meurt*. For the N.R.F. Gide also omitted a paragraph which stated that he was not having this limited edition reprinted soon. Hoy argues that this was obviously a fabrication on Gide's part in order to set the mind of his elderly English correspondent at rest. It is more probable that Gide was less conniving than Hoy allows, and had simply submitted a draft copy of his letter for publication at the N.R.F., having forgotten that he had made changes in the letter actually sent.

significantly uses "pourquoi je les publie" where he had formerly used "écrire".[6] Some years later Roger Martin du Gard was to insist on the distinction between "écrire" and "publier". He added a note to a letter he had written to André Gide in 1926. In the note he states rigorously that he had not discouraged his correspondent from *writing* his autobiography. On the contrary. But he *had* discouraged Gide from having it published in his lifetime or soon afterwards.[7] When Martin du Gard said that it was to avoid hurting Madeleine that he was discouraging publication, Gide confessed that he hoped that a scandal might bring her back to him, after their rupture of 1918.[8] It is also Martin du Gard who speaks of the strength of purpose which lay behind *Si le grain ne meurt* and others of Gide's works. On the eve of a birthday, Gide has spoken of the eighty-first year of his "emploi sur cette terre". Martin du Gard notes: "L'expression *'l'emploi' sur cette terre* n'est pas venue par hasard sous la plume de Gide: elle exprime ce sentiment qui lui a fait publier *Corydon* et *Si le grain* et la correspondance avec Claudel, —à savoir qu'il a un rôle, une mission à remplir; et que son talent, l'autorité qu'il s'est acquise, doivent, avant tout, servir à lutter contre les préjugés de la morale conformiste, pour soustraire les homosexuels à l'inique condamnation qui pèse sur eux."[9]

One gains another insight into the purpose of Gide's autobiography by examining its title. Its biblical source is John 12: 24, and on the title page of the original edition there appeared the quotation, " . . . après qu'on l'a jeté dans la terre il demeure seul; mais s'il meurt il porte beaucoup de fruits." Gide had hunted several days for a title for his work. He rejected *Mémoires, Souvenirs,* and *Confessions* before hesitating between two more imaginative ones. On the ground that it narrowed the sense of the work, he rejected *Et Ego* in favour of *Si le grain ne meurt,* which, he felt, widened it.[10] Presumably he meant that thanks to the proverbial quality of his metaphorical title, the plea for tolerance in the work would be accepted as more widely applicable than just to himself. But in the title, just what was

6. This short preface is published in *Oeuvres complètes,* x: 453-4, and in Lejeune, *L'Autobiographie en France,* pp. 192-3.
7. *Correspondance André Gide-Roger Martin du Gard, 1913-1951,* 2 vols. (Paris, 1968), i: 657. Martin du Gard's own discretion about publication of his personal papers is well known.
8. Reported by Jean Delay in the *Correspondance Gide-Martin du Gard,* i: 68-9.
9. *Ibid.,* ii: 469.
10. *Journal,* le 11 janvier 1917, p. 612.

the dying seed supposed to represent? Is it, as George Painter has suggested, his puritanical past which had died when he fell ill at Biskra and defied his heritage by indulging in sensual pleasure?[11] Among the fruits of this harvest could be found, incidentally, *Les Nourritures terrestres.* Or must the wild oats he sowed at Biskra die in order for him to grow in his marriage to his cousin, promised on the final page? Or is it a past of longer duration, continuing up to the time of writing, which must die in order that he may "begin a new life of freedom and serenity"?[12] Is it, perhaps, Gide himself who must die, a martyr for the cause of homosexuality, in order that an age of tolerance may be born? He seemed obsessed with the prospect of his own death during the years of composition,[13] and when around the time of general distribution of the work he set out for Africa, he felt that it was literally the end of his life. The ambiguity of the title must have delighted Gide.[14] In any case, the writing of the work itself, the commitment of the past to paper, was for Gide a purgative process. Events in his life became complete only when transformed into art; and in a certain sense, this transformation is something of a ritualistic burial with the erection of a permanent monument — the work itself. But this is true of all Gide's works.

None of the above theories is entirely satisfactory, for they all to varying degrees stray too far from the biblical source and Gide's particular interpretation of it. Traditionally, the verse is construed as meaning that only through self-mortification can one attain a truly full life. The following verse (John 12: 25), which Gide considered essential to the understanding of the passage, emphasizes the rewards, even in this life, that paradoxically result from self-abnegation. In *Numquid et tu . . . ?* Gide explains the verse this way: "Celui qui aime sa vie, son âme, — qui protège sa personnalité, qui soigne sa figure dans ce monde — la perdra; mais celui-là qui en fera l'abandon, la rendra vraiment vivante, lui assurera la vie éternelle; non point la vie futurement éternelle, mais la fera déjà, dès à présent, vivre à

---

11. Painter, *André Gide: A Critical Biography*, p. 79.
12. Enid Starkie's interpretation in her *André Gide,* p. 38.
13. See, for instance, Gide's reference to his own prospective death written in the *Journal* only three days after selecting his title, le 21 janvier 1917, p. 615.
14. At least one interpretation annoyed him: "N'y va-t-on jusqu'à voir dans ce titre *'Si le grain ne meurt'* une apologie 'gidienne' de la pourriture!" writes Gide to Mauriac in October 1927, *Correspondance André Gide-François Mauriac, 1912-1950* (Paris, 1971), p. 74.

même l'éternité."[15] When he makes his confessions, then, Gide is performing an act of exceptional humiliation, which could, he believes, bring a fuller life to generations of others and immeasurable happiness to himself even within his own lifetime. The seed that must die is his own reputation—which will bring a harvest of freer, happier people. Of his own fulfilment he says: "Résurrection dans la vie totale. Oubli de tout bonheur particulier. O réintégration parfaite!"[16] The superficially egotistical gesture of writing about oneself is, in fact, an altruistic one, involving personal martyrdom. Only secondarily, through the happiness of others, does it bring satisfaction to its author — but this in great measure.

The fact that martyrdom thus becomes a curious key to Gide's happiness leads critics like Mario Praz to speak of the sado-masochistic side to Gide's notion of writing "confessions".[17] But his biblical title gives evidence that he viewed his project almost reverently. There is no conscious Gidean irony at play in the selection of such a title for a work with a non-biblical thesis; and when, many years later, readers could identify Gide himself in his portrait of the aged Thésée, serenely proud of his life's accomplishments in the interests of others, the world acknowledged that the seed had not died in vain.

The writing and publishing history of *Si le grain ne meurt* furnishes some useful information about the hesitancy that even the more uninhibited of autobiographers can feel. Gide's *Journal* and *Correspondance* (with Martin du Gard) and Mme Théo van Rysselberghe's notebooks provide us with almost as useful an account of the gestation of his autobiography as does the *Journal des Faux-monnayeurs* for Gide's novel. And an examination of the manuscript in the Bibliothèque Jacques Doucet verifies Gide's comments about "hésitation", "retours", and "reprises" in the composition. We know too that Gide worked from notes which he filed chronologically year by year for the years 1874 to 1900. According to Jean Delay these notes include mention of turning-points, recollections in cryptic form, some rough drafts, and even some texts that never found their way into either *Si le grain ne meurt* or the *Journal*.

With the exception of Chapters Nine and Ten, Gide appears to have written the work in the successive order of the published chapters, beginning with his earliest recollections. On March

15. *Journal*, le 4 mars 1916, p. 594.
16. *Ibid.*
17. Mario Praz, *The Romantic Agony*, 2nd ed. (London, 1951), p. 366.

10, 1916, he was having difficulty with the account in Chapter One of his walks with his father in the Luxembourg Gardens.[18] By mid-December he had written the rue de Lecat episode at the beginning of Chapter Five, the very part that had stopped him short in October. He was then ready to read the first four chapters to his wife, while giving her the extremely personal beginning of the fifth to read herself.[19] This chapter was finished by mid-January 1917, when he read her the full version. [20] By mid-March, in spite of difficulties in concentration, he had completed the conversation with Bernard Tissaudier (actually Albert Jalaguier) towards the middle of Chapter Seven.[21] Marginal comments in Gide's hand in the manuscript indicate that Gide completed the chapter between the 20th of May and the 4th of June, and was working on Chapter Eight almost daily from the 8th to the 23rd of June, around which time it was completed. On the evening of September 23, 1917, he read aloud to Madeleine the part written in the early summer (presumably the latter part of Chapter Seven and all of Chapter Eight). The next day he began Chapter Nine, with the death of Anna Shackleton.[22] Emotional preoccupation as well as his translation of *Antony and Cleopatra* prevented him from working well on the "Mémoires" in the fall. By this time, though, between March 1916 and September 1917, he had written the first eight chapters of his "Mémoires". His work had not been regular, nor had he found it easy or entirely satisfying;[23] nevertheless, this accomplishment in bulk alone is not to be scoffed at.

A footnote to the first chapter of Part Two indicates that this part was not begun until the spring of 1919.[24] On the 29th of April, Gide read to Mme Théo van Rysselberghe and Madame Mayrisch at the latter's home in Luxembourg the early chapters of Part One. Mme van Rysselberghe's account of this reading is informative enough to deserve quoting:

---

18. *Journal,* le 10 mars 1916, pp. 547-8. Gide may have been writing a part of what is now *Si le grain ne meurt* even earlier. See the *Journal,* le 21 juin 1910, p. 305, for mention of writing about En-Barka, Mohammed, and "le petit de Sousse".

19. *Journal,* le 19 et 23 décembre 1916, pp. 585-6.

20. *Journal,* le 18 janvier 1917, p. 612.

21. *Journal,* le 22 mars 1917, p. 622.

22. *Journal,* le 23 et 24 septembre 1917, p. 632.

23. See *Journal 1889-1939* entries pp. 547-8, 551-2, 572, 584, 585-6, 615, 619-20, 632.

24. *Si le grain ne meurt,* p. 549.

— A nous deux, il lit des fragments des Mémoires (*Si le grain
ne meurt*), qu'il a menés jusqu'à l'âge de dix-huit ans. Jean
Schlumberger lui avait objecté un air de dessiner sa figure avec
trop de complaisance par le choix des anecdotes; seuls quelques
commentaires, qui soulignent la signification de certains traits
de son enfance, nous paraissent justifier ce reproche. Il se
défend, du reste, de choisir, décidé à dire tout ce qui surnage
dans sa mémoire, avec la plus scrupuleuse, la plus entière
vérité. Il nous demande aussi notre avis sur l'opportunité des
indécences, ou plutôt des indiscrétions? Mais il nous paraît que
tout est important, même si cela doit fournir des armes contre
lui. Tu lui demandes: "Il ne vous en coûte pas d'avouer certaines
choses?" Il dit nettement: "Pas du tout. Tout ce qui fait partie
de la respectabilité: situation, décoration, etc., et que je
compromets ainsi n'arrive pas à me faire envie." Il compte
donner d'abord de *Si le grain ne meurt* une édition restreinte (6 à
7 exemplaires), rien pour le public. Je lui demande s'il y aura
une seconde partie: "Oui, dit-il, et toute différente, moins
complète peut-être, et nettement présentée comme une
défense." Nous sommes navrées d'en entendre si peu. Il arrête
au moment où il parle d'Uzès. Nous sommes comme grisées par
un tel plaisir, et lui aussi sent l'excellence de ce qu'il vient de
lire. Il résume notre état ainsi: "Comme ce serait triste d'être
bête!" [. . .][25]

In the summer of 1920 Gide was writing of his 1893 trip to
Algeria with Paul-Albert Laurens (most of Part Two, Chapter
One), and in November was working on what he called the
"chapitres intermédiaires" — the present Chapters Nine and
Ten of Part One.[26] He appears to have picked up his manuscript
again at the point in Chapter Nine immediately after the death
of Anna Shackleton. On the 6th of November, Mme van Rysselberghe, who was staying with him in the Villa Montmo-
rency, wrote, "Il me lit le chapitre sur lequel il a peiné hier
soir, celui où il est question d'Albert Démarest. Non seulement
il permet toutes les remarques, mais il aime qu'on lui en
fasse."[27] Three days later, he read aloud the passage on Marc de
la Nux written the night before, and spoke of all the notes he
had accumulated on this "attachante figure".[28] On February
23, 1921, at the van Rysselberghe property at Saint-Clair, he

25. Maria van Rysselberghe, *Les Cahiers de la Petite Dame: Notes pour l'histoire
authentique d'André Gide, 1918-1929* (Paris, 1973), p. 22.
26. *Journal*, le 1er novembre 1920, p. 685.
27. *Cahiers de la Petite Dame*, p. 53.
28. *Ibid.*, p. 54.

read his passages on "la cousine Feuchères, le milieu Heredia, Mallarmé".[29] He had just polished up at Cuverville in January a printable version of "les deux chapitres supplémentaires de la première partie de mes Mémoires".[30]

Madame van Rysselberghe does not clarify whether the passage from Part Two, Chapter Two (following Gide's African meeting with Oscar Wilde), which he aired for her on April 3, 1921, was freshly written or not.[31] She merely states that she had not yet heard this part, and that Gide was particularly concerned with its success. He must have been relieved and excited by Ernst Robert Curtius's enthusiastic response to the "dernière partie", when he read it aloud to him at the Mayrisches' home at Colpach in June.[32] This was not the complete Second Part, since it was not until the 14th day of July at Cuverville that Gide announced that he had finished the "troisième chapitre de la seconde partie" (which would be published in the format of two chapters).[33] On the 9th day of August, again at Colpach, he read aloud the final pages of *Si le grain ne meurt* to the general admiration of some assembled friends. Mme van Rysselberghe, however, was later the same day daring enough to inform him that they had found some obscurity in his motivation for marriage on the final page.[34] In high spirits after a stimulating evening, Gide immediately

29. *Ibid.*, p. 69.
30. *Journal*, le 26 janvier 1921, p. 690. One must assume that Gide had suffered a change of heart over the structuring of these two chapters some time in January; for in the *Journal* entry for the 1st of January, he was using the singular form "chapitre intermédiaire" to speak of this section. There is also evidence that he was contemplating even further divisions; for in the manuscript he begins the section that is found on page 518 of the Pléiade edition (his year of philosophy) with the query "Nouveau chapitre?"
31. *Cahiers de la Petite Dame*, p. 71.
32. *Ibid.*, p. 89.
33. *Journal, 1889-1939*, p. 696.
34. *Cahiers de la Petite Dame*, p. 92. Mme van Rysselberghe and her friends were not alone in their puzzlement. In each of my classes where we have studied *Si le grain ne meurt*, I have found several students totally bewildered by the announcement of this marriage only a few pages after the narrator's crystal-clear confession of having been a remorseless homosexual. The most satisfactory succinct explanation I have found is that of the psychiatrist-biographer Jean Delay: "Quand disparut avec elle [Mme Paul Gide] un passé de contrainte, il éprouva jusqu'à l'angoisse l'ivresse de la liberté. Et c'est alors que par un étrange retour, où se révèle sa complication, il redemande en mariage Madeleine Rondeaux qui, cette fois, crut devoir accepter." "Gide ou l'expérience de soi", p. 85. It is the same kind of fear of total liberty which motivates Gide's heroine Isabelle to destroy her chances for freedom in the *récit* of the same name.

conceded that she was right and made plans to remedy the situation. On the 19th day of August, la Petite Dame told Gide that she thought that Lord Alfred Douglas would press charges on reading his book. Gide's response? Of course he would, but the opportunity to express the truth about Wilde and Douglas was worth it to him.[35]

By this time (the summer of 1921) Gide had, of course, published the first eight chapters of *Si le grain ne meurt* — those completed in 1917. He had submitted them to the Imprimerie Sainte-Catherine at Bruges, which had for a long time been the regular printing house for all the publications of the Nouvelle Revue Française. Printing had been completed on May 15, 1920. On the title page there had been no mention either of a publishing house or that this might be Volume One of a two-volume set. Only twelve copies were printed of this 1920 private edition.

In the summer of 1921, Gide wrote to Martin du Gard that he had entrusted the rest of *Si le grain ne meurt* (Chapters Nine and Ten of Part One and all of Part Two) to M. Edouard Verbeke (of the Imprimerie Sainte-Catherine).[36] Mme van Rysselberghe pinpoints the date. On the 25th of August, she writes: "Nous venons de passer deux jours à Bruxelles: Gide devait y rencontrer l'imprimeur de Bruges pour lui confier la dernière partie de *Si le grain ne meurt*."[37] Thirteen copies were printed, and the title page acknowledged that this was the "Deuxième Volume", giving the publication data as simply Paris, 1921. Printing was not completed until the day before Christmas of that year.

It is interesting that Gide had been ready to send his first eight chapters to the printer even before completing the subsequent narrative. One might believe that, recognizing the relatively innocuous and sometimes idyllic nature of these "souvenirs d'enfance et de jeunesse", Gide might have been thinking of a future republication of this volume more or less as it was, with no one the wiser that there was a second more controversial one. However, a different light is shed on Gide's intentions by the history of some crucial complications in the contract for the private edition.[38] In the summer of 1918 Gide had been

35. *Cahiers de la Petite Dame*, p. 99.
36. *Correspondance Gide-Martin du Gard*, I: 173. The letter is dated "août ou septembre 1921". Gide misspelled the gentleman's name as "Verbecke", although he had known him since at least 1908. Contrariwise, Gide consistently *omitted* the "c" from Shackleton.
37. *Cahiers de la Petite Dame*, p. 102.
38. See François Chapon, "Note sur l'édition du second *Corydon*", *Bulletin du Bibliophile* I (1971): 1-9.

thinking of printing no more than four or five copies of the chapters that had been completed, as we have seen, in 1917. He was hoping that this luxury edition with illustrations might be backed financially by M. Jacques Doucet, who had already bought some of Gide's manuscripts for his "bibliothèque littéraire". The uncertainty of the outcome of the war, unfortunately, was not auspicious for such a venture. Unable to draw up a satisfactory agreement, Doucet withdrew his participation. A few months later when the allies' victory seemed secure, Doucet again brought up the subject only to discover that the offer of publication had been accepted by Lady Rothermere, who had translated Gide's *Prométhée mal enchaîné*. She was also the patroness of the young Paul Méral, who was rumoured to be founding a new periodical to be call *La Roue*.[39] All concerned felt that portions of Gide's autobiography would enhance the new *revue*.

Doucet, disappointed not to be involved in the project, asked at least to be allowed to subscribe to a copy of the private edition of the "Mémoires" at a price to be agreed upon by the interested parties. The response was affirmative: a sixth copy would be printed and reserved for him provided he would associate himself with Lady Rothermere to share equally the expenses of a new revised and enlarged edition of *Corydon*. On the historic date November 11, 1918, Gide, Doucet, Lady Rothermere, and Paul Méral all met in Méral's apartment to negotiate the contract.[40] Gide was to provide his backers with copies of his "Mémoires" and the revised *Corydon,* as well as a copy of the first edition of *Corydon*. Moreover, Gide was to promise never to publish a commercial edition of these works without modifying them. The recipients of the contracted editions would keep them secret, although selections could be printed in Méral's periodical or in another of Gide's choice. Eventually, the deal fell through. Gide himself took up Lady Rothermere's share of the expense in publishing *Corydon*; and according to a letter from Méral to Gide, he and Lady Rothermere bought the rights

39. Paul Méral's real name was Gouchtenaer. M. Claude Martin informs us that the Vieux-Colombier had staged Méral's avant-garde dramatic poem, *Le Dit des jeux du monde,* in 1918. See *Cahiers de la Petite Dame,* p. 422, n. 15. Mme van Rysselberghe describes Gide's mirth on quoting Méral's comment: "Si Alissa avait épousé Jérôme, elle serait devenue étroite et mesquine comme Amélie [of *La Symphonie pastorale*]!!" *Ibid.*, p. 18. As for Lady Lilian Rothermere, her name at least is echoed in the Lady Lilian Griffith of *Les Faux-monnayeurs.*

40. A lot of writing was going on that day; this is also the date of the first entry in the *Cahiers* of Mme van Rysselberghe.

to publish a limited edition of *Si le grain ne meurt.* [41]

What is interesting in this account is not so much the outcome of the negotiations as the information it provides about Gide's attitude to *Si le grain ne meurt.* It would appear that at this point he was determined that even those innocuous early chapters should not be published in a commercial edition. He consistently associated the function and importance of his autobiography with that of *Corydon,* and was ready to provide an exceptional twin birth for the two of them, either at great expense to himself or—worse still—at the cost of prostituting his art with a promise never to publish them again in volume form unless modified. One finds this latter stipulation contrary to all the ideology of freedom which Gide regularly preached—most particularly in the very works in question. Our only conclusion can be that, torn between an urge to publish them in his lifetime and a fear of a premature general revelation of their contents, he was ready to resort to this financially and morally expensive compromise.

As for the private edition of 1920-1, Charles Du Bos has quite rightly pointed out that it contains many details which have been altered in subsequent versions. [42] Du Bos finds the changes regrettable, on the grounds that Gide was attempting to render his style more banal and impersonal in later editions. Regrettable or not, the most noticeable of the modifications have been the changes of many proper names. The real ones, which are fine in a private edition, could in a commercial edition result in hurt feelings in family or close friends, or even libel suits from sensitive acquaintances. The names were already changed in the long "fragments" published in the *Nouvelle Revue Française.* The first six chapters, only moderately abridged, appeared one per issue in the February, March, May,

---

41. Mme van Rysselberghe records that on September 13, 1919, Gide had just made up his mind about the details of printing the first edition of *Si le grain ne meurt*: "il y en aura douze exemplaires seulement: un pour Doucet, deux pour Lady Rothermere et Gouchtenaer (s'ils continuent à faire partie de la combinaison pécuniaire), un pour lui, un pour Jean Schlumberger (qu'il considère présentement comme son exécuteur testamentaire), un pour toi [Mme Mayrisch], un pour moi. Les autres, c'est la réserve, pour l'imprévu auquel il fait toujours une part." *Cahiers de la Petite Dame,* p. 38. One of the reserve copies was sought after by the Belgian bibliophile Dr. Willy Schuermans. *Ibid.,* p. 426. A copy sold for 5300 francs in the auction of 1925. *Ibid.,* p. 430, n. 158.

42. Du Bos, *Dialogue avec André Gide,* pp. 38-9n. Gide had lent Du Bos a copy of the private edition soon after its publication. It is from this edition that Du Bos quotes in his early "entretien". See my Appendix B for notes on many of the variants in this edition.

November, and December numbers of 1920, and January 1921. Chapter Ten appeared much later in the issue of January 1924. Through the pages of his own N.R.F., then, Gide first satisfied his urge to publish publicly the story of his life; but without Part Two the basic purpose behind publishing the work remained unfulfilled.

One is naturally led to ask which version came first, the N.R.F. *fragments* or the private edition. Collating the N.R.F. *fragments* with the manuscript and the private edition suggests that Gide corrected the proofs for the *fragments* of the first six chapters before those of the private edition. Some wording from the manuscript which was modified in the private edition remains in the N.R.F. version. In Chapter Six, for instance, in an account of a meal at Val-Richer, there is a partial sentence which reads in the manuscript and the N.R.F. (January 1921): "et durant un long temps on ne voyait plus un visage." The private edition has: "et durant un long temps sur tout le tour de la table, l'invité ne voyait plus un visage." The definitive version (in the Pléiade edition, p. 470) is the same as the private edition, except that after "l'invité" we find the clause "que j'étais". Some arguments could be brought forward here that in the first *revised* version (i.e., in the private edition) Gide is drawing the reader to the point of view of a guest at the table rather than that of a mysterious "on" placed anywhere within view of the scene. In the definitive edition, he is rendering the whole scene even more personal with an additional clause which serves to remind us that the guest whose point of view the reader is sharing is the young — and awkward—André Gide. This variant at least, then, would succeed in discounting Du Bos's argument about Gide's impersonalization in later revisions; but for our purposes here, it serves to show that Gide either revised the N.R.F. proofs first or overlooked prior revisions of the private edition when correcting for the N.R.F. It is possible, of course, that for one reason or another he kept the two proof revisions quite separate from each other. If he did not, we are permitted to say that the *fragments* of the N.R.F. antedate the rare private edition, and are in fact the first publication of *Si le grain ne meurt* — a "pré-édition" rather than a "première édition".

Several more editions appear before the one for general distribution. "Hérédité" in *Morceaux choisis* (Paris, Nouvelle Revue Française, 1921) is a page from Chapter One. There are "fragments" from Chapters One to Three in *André Gide* (Paris, Crès, Bibliothèque de l'Adolescence, 1921), and yet another extract (part of Chapter Nine) appears as a preface to R. Doré and R.

Simonson, *Les Livres d'André Gide* (Paris, Champion, 1923). In 1924 Edouard Champion also published a limited edition (130 copies) of a tidily handwritten version of Chapter Ten which Gide tells of copying for him.[43]

In 1925, quite ironically, an edition for English schoolboys appeared at the Clarendon Press. It contained extracts from the first three chapters, more abridged than the *N.R.F. fragments,* but following the variants of their text. It would appear that the Clarendon editor, V.F. Boyson, did not have access to any other edition. He wrote a short essay supposedly suitable for young students on "André Gide and His Work". This is a syrupy eulogy on the uniqueness and beauty of Gide's prose. Gide himself contributed an "avant-propos" addressed to the students. In this he expressed surprise at any interest his story might have for British youth. He underlined, however, the importance of mutual international understanding, regretting never having studied in Britain, and not being able to speak English. With an example of his own frustration in once not having been able to communicate with an agreeable English army officer, he concludes by encouraging the French and English students to learn each other's language. Boyson's notes for the school edition are the usual sort: explanations of difficult grammar and vocabulary, identification of geographical and literary allusions. He thoughtfully included on the inside back cover two maps of the north-east corner of Le Calvados and the southern portion of Le Gard. A *lexique* and several pages of phrases and idioms complete the edition. One cannot help wondering what Mr. Boyson's attitude to his school edition would have been had he seen the *rest* of *Si le grain ne meurt.* Indeed, what *was* his reaction when a year later he must have seen the full commercial version? The existence of the Boyson edition should not pass unnoticed in any study of the ironies in Gide's career.

The three-volume edition published by Gallimard, "la pre-mière édition intégrale mise dans le commerce", was first distributed in October or November 1926.[44] The printing had been limited to 6,050 copies which, dated 1924, had been

43. *Journal,* le 23 juin 1924, p. 786. The title page of the photocopied manuscript indicates that it was printed on the 20th of July.
44. The Arnold Naville *Bibliographie des écrits d'André Gide 1891-1952* (Paris, 1949) claims October. Talvart and Place vouch for November. At any rate, Gide told Mme van Rysselberghe on October 19, 1926, "Je vais sans doute lâcher bientôt *Si le grain ne meurt*, ouvrir la cage," *Cahiers de la Petite Dame,* p. 290. The reviews started appearing on the 4th of December.

sitting in the warehouse waiting for Gide to decide the right moment for distribution. Gallimard had consented to publish both *Corydon* and *Si le grain ne meurt* on seeing them at Pontigny in the summer of 1922.[45] On October 21, 1922, Gide told Mme van Rysselberghe that both works were being printed, but that he would like to complete his novel before distribution.[46] By the time he was leaving for Africa, he decided that he should put off the release of *Si le grain ne meurt* until his return. It would seem cowardly to publish it and run.[47] By the actual time of release, sufficient time had gone by for Gide to have had serious doubts about its title;[48] and Gallimard was obliged to add "une bande avec changement de prix".[49]

Gide tells of correcting the proofs for this edition in December 1922 and May 1923.[50] In September 1928, he would again be correcting proofs, this time for the so-called definitive edition, the publication date of which had not yet been specified.[51] This one-volume edition, with more variants since the edition of 1924, was, in fact, printed in November 1928, and went on sale in March 1929. Precisely thirteen years had passed between Gide's writing of his first word and the publication of his "édition définitive"; thirty years had passed since the work's conception. An autobiographer's conscience does not have an easy task.

It is characteristic of literary autobiographers that they should take mild criticism of their autobiography more personally than the blackest of condemnations of their fiction, poetry, or drama. For in the case of autobiographies it is the very soul of the writer which is being attacked more obviously than his literary talent. Gide, who had written to be accused, must have been eagerly apprehensive about the reviews. One early appraisal of the first chapter, based on its appearance in the February 1920 issue of the N.R.F., could not be considered representative. (The anonymous critic of the *Revue Romande*, le 15 mars 1920, saw a precocious child and lovely images in the work, and prophesied anthologizing for the kaleidoscope episode.) It would be, rather, the critics who had read the full

45. *Cahiers de la Petite Dame*, p. 147.
46. *Ibid.*, p. 159.
47. *Ibid.*, p. 201.
48. In the summer of 1923 on the grounds that it was too "formulé". *Ibid.*, p. 186.
49. *Ibid.*, p. 292.
50. *Journal,* pp. 746, 757.
51. *Ibid.*, p. 887.

35

work who would steer the public reaction. The first of these, Maurice Martin du Gard, in *Les Nouvelles Littéraires*, le 4 décembre 1926, admired the work, stating at the same time that it was not for hypocrites or little girls. He thought that the portraits of Pierre Louÿs, Oscar Wilde, and Lord Alfred Douglas, and the death of Madame Gide would be the parts that would last. So far so good.

Fernand Vandérem's article in *La Revue de France*, le 15 décembre 1926, was longer.[52] After a chatty introduction in which he wonders how so many of his contemporaries find the time to write memoirs, he finds that Gide's consistent domination of the work is a link between *Si le grain ne meurt* and Rousseau's *Confessions*. It is this common characteristic which distinguishes both works from memoirs. He insists on the young Gide's lack of extraordinary qualities, finding many pages devoid of interest. Vandérem does not even see anything exceptional in the account of Gide's suspension from the Ecole Alsacienne! He is happy to see evidence in *Si le grain ne meurt* of the philosophical origins of Gide's thought, sources he had always suspected were there. He likes best the Algerian part, thinking that the literary salons were handled better by Jules Renard. He concludes by admitting, though, that he does not understand *why* Gide chose to confess. In other words, in an otherwise quite perceptive article, Vandérem, by finding Gide's autobiography neither very original nor very pernicious, proved that he had missed the fundamental purpose of the book.

Paul Souday in *Le Temps*, le 23 décembre 1926, accused Gide of being too vague and general, long-winded and boring. His opinion is that an author has a right to be scandalous, provided he remains interesting. Rousseau was successful; Gide is not. Contrary to Vandérem, Souday likes best the parts on literary people. In a final note Souday expresses admiration for the *Journal des Faux-monnayeurs* which he had also just read.[53]

Gide's colleague at the N.R.F., Félix Bertaux, reviewed the

52. The article forms part of the column "Les Lettres et la vie", pp. 733-8.
53. Souday's review is part of a column entitled "Les Livres", which in this issue was mainly devoted to Gide and Wilde. Gide's *Journal* reveals *passim* that his relations with the influential critic were uneven. The entry for le 14 décembre 1923, is particularly telling:
"—Comment Souday est-il avec vous?
—Il a été successivement froid et bouillant suivant qu'il m'a cru royaliste ou républicain. Depuis qu'il a compris que je n'étais ni l'un ni l'autre, il est devenu tiède; il m'accorde une certaine valeur, en tant qu'artiste, mais 'comme penseur' trouve que je ne vaux rien." P. 771.

volume for the February 1927 issue.[54] He discusses the general question of "pudeur", which he sees as having evolved surprisingly slowly if one looks at its progress from Montaigne through Stendhal to Gide. He finds affinities between Montaigne's and Gide's ideas on enjoyment of one's being. He appreciates Gide's need to publish the work as a public service. The question of liberating the public from prejudices, Bertaux points out, is not private but universal. If Gide had not acted, who would have? And, we may add, if an N.R.F. reviewer had not appreciated the purpose of *Si le grain ne meurt,* who could have?

Guy Bernard in *La Revue Nouvelle* saw *Si le grain ne meurt* as essentially moral.[55] He found, just as he had hoped, that the publication cemented his ideas of a complete Gidean personality. It also presented general truths, showing the oppositions between flesh and the soul, pleasure and love, evil and good. As kind and correct as this review is, though, its general effect is rather bland.

On the other hand, Gide's *bête noire* at the *Mercure de France,* Jean de Gourmont, was true to form.[56] He called the work "cette morose confession puritaine", snidely emphasizing that for Gide a trip without a Bible was a triumph, and that the religious aspects of the book would hurt Gide's Nietzschean image. The work showed, he said, that Gide's God was far from dead. He did understand clearly, though, that Gide was preaching the normality of homosexuality, and that to this extent the work was a rare human document. He points out that while homosexuality may be a good *artistic* spark, it is not a very good *philosophical* one, quite rightly but unpleasantly classing Whitman and Gide as "poètes" rather than "philosophes". He found the family details dull but probably exact, and some of the literary portraits fascinating but recognizably unjust.

Two reviews published in foreign periodicals were among the most sympathetic. René Lalou, in a Dutch periodical, saw the vastness of Gide's enterprise, noting that the author's conviction brought this to the realm of great *international* literature. He describes it as containing "à la fois un récit, une autobiographie, une interprétation de cette confession, l'analyse d'une passion tenue généralement pour anormale, enfin la révélation

54. Félix Bertaux, *"Si le grain ne meurt"*, Nouvelle Revue Française, 14ᵉ année, février 1927, pp. 258-63.
55. In a section of reviews called "Divers", le 15 février 1927, pp. 55-6.
56. In the "Littérature" section of the "Revue de la quinzaine", *Mercure de France*, le 1ᵉʳ mars 1927, pp. 388-91.

d'une doctrine que l'on pourra juger évangélique ou hérétique."[57] He concludes by finding that Gide's admirable originality lies in the evolving combination of certainty and anxiety which Gide traces with unusual daring and even rarer lucidity. Jean Cassou, writing in a Spanish periodical, praises the book for its explanation of man's complexity.[58] Gide attempted honesty in his self-portrait, and the world is better for it. Cassou goes so far as to say that we witness here one of the major triumphs of human intelligence. As was so often the case, this future Nobel Prize winner was receiving his acclaim from abroad, albeit this time from French writers.

By mid-May 1927, about six months after the general distribution of *Si le grain ne meurt,* Gide was able to tally up the score on at least these eight reviews which he or his secretary clipped and filed.[59] One review had missed the point entirely, and two had been unnecessarily unkind. Of the three others published in France, two were helpful without being influentially enthusiastic, and the third was written for Gide's own N.R.F. The praise in the reviews published abroad would carry little or no weight in France; but Gide could take solace in the fact that his subject was certainly international, and already his book was being discussed outside France. He had, of course, no reason to worry about sales: *Si le grain ne meurt* would enjoy a *succès de scandale.*

57. René Lalou, "Lettres parisiennes XIII", *Het Fransche Boek*, April 1927, p. 113. René Lalou would write a preface for Gide's *Dostoïevski* later the same year.
58. Jean Cassou, "Si no muere el grano", *La Gaceta Literaria,* 15 maio 1927.
59. The file of reviews is held in the Fonds Gide at the Bibliothèque Jacques Doucet. They have all been dated, but do not necessarily retain their page references. I hasten to add that I have made no attempt to give a complete survey of the critical reaction to *Si le grain ne meurt.* I have, rather, used the *dossier* to illustrate some of the representative views of which Gide was certainly aware.

3
The Structure of an Autobiography

WHEN we read *Si le grain ne meurt* today in a standard current edition, we are at first struck by the imbalance in the length of its two parts. André Gide often conceived works in two parts, as in the case of each of *Les Cahiers d'André Walter, La Porte étroite, L'Ecole des femmes,* and *Robert.* Sometimes (most notably in *La Symphonie pastorale*) his impatience to complete a work and get on with the next overcame his desire for classical symmetry, resulting in the second part's being shorter than the first. But in none of these works is the imbalance as glaring as the proportion of ten chapters to two in *Si le grain ne meurt.* My account of the gestation of the work has suggested that the imbalance was intentional; the leisurely first part was meant to emphasize the mainly unexceptional nature of Gide's youth in preparation for the dramatic revelations of the second part.[1] What Gide has done here is to take a lesson from fiction. He has structured his work in such a way that through the development of the first part the reader is drawn into such close contact with the personality of the young Gide that he is ready to linger with him over the most commonplace of remembrances. The reader is made to

---

1. Gide *did* contemplate continuing *Si le grain ne meurt.* However, it was no accident that his first edition stopped where it did. Before he had completed the work we now possess, his aesthetic sense must have told him that this form would well suit his purposes. See, for instance, his *Journal,* le 26 janvier 1921, p. 690; le 28 mai 1921, p. 695; le 14 juillet 1921, p. 696.

feel that a climax awaits him further on, and that this climax is not necessarily, as is the case with most literary autobiographers, just the publication or success of a literary work. Gide's skill in building suspense here is entirely professional. The device he uses is the familiar one of foreshadowing. And he uses the device rhythmically. The first occurrence is on the very first page; Gide's account of his "games" with the *concierge*'s son is followed by promise of further sexual revelations: "Je sais de reste le tort que je me fais en racontant ceci *et ce qui va suivre*; je pressens le parti qu'on en pourra tirer contre moi" (Pléiade, p. 349, italics mine). Shortly after, he presents his friendship with little Mouton in physical terms: "Je ne me souviens pas que nous fissions autre chose que de nous promener, la main dans la main, sans rien dire" (pp. 352-3). He will come back to sexual questions later when he dwells on the sources of sexual excitement in his childhood, mentioning particularly two usually innocuous works by George Sand and Mme de Ségur (pp. 386-7). Almost immediately after, at the beginning of Chapter Three, follows the account of Gide's suspension from the Ecole Alsacienne for having been found masturbating in class (pp. 390-1). He says of the delicate Russian boy for whom he was gallantly ready to go to battle: "Il y en avait un [camarade] pour qui je m'étais épris d'une véritable passion" (p. 404). And he was positively overpowered by one self-assured and stunningly clad boy at the children's costume-ball: "Et pour achever ma confusion, voici que, tout à coup, je tombai amoureux, oui, positivement amoureux, d'un garçonnet un peu plus âgé que moi, qui devait me laisser un souvenir ébloui de sa sveltesse, de sa grâce et de sa volubilité" (p. 406). Very soon after, we have the account of Barnett's assorted prowesses: "Tout son être éclatait de joie, de santé et d'une espèce de turbulence intérieure qui le faisait inventer sans cesse quelque excentricité pleine de risque, par quoi il s'auréolait de prestige à mes yeux, et positivement m'enthousiasmait" (pp. 407-8). Barnett's most memorable public performance appears to have occurred on the first day at the *pension*: "il se campa tout au milieu [du petit jardin], le torse glorieusement rejeté en arrière, et sous nos yeux à tous, en hauteur, il pissa." All of Gide's youthful friendships (after the *concierge*'s son) seem to have been innocent; but the use of such expressions as "la main dans la main", "véritable passion", "positivement amoureux", and "le torse glorieusement rejeté en arrière", which denote physical attraction to other boys, should not pass unnoticed. Most autobiographers have had memorable attractions to other young people; few, however, have dared — or bothered — to describe them in these terms. But few have been writing with the same purpose as Gide.

This sort of allusion is significantly absent throughout the pages surrounding the important rue de Lecat episode in Chapter Five, although a general allusion to the devil occurs at the end of Chapter Four: "Décidément le diable me guettait" (p. 430). The ambiguous despairing cry of "Je ne suis pas pareil aux autres!" (p. 439) is placed strategically about one-third of the way through the book, and encourages even tired readers to plunge on.

The summer of 1884 was dominated by Gide's attachment to his neighbour at Val-Richer, Lionel de R. (really François de Witt). Their relationship took on many of the romantic qualities of Hugo's early years with Juliette Drouet, or Emma Bovary's with Rodolphe: "Nous nous donnions de vrais rendez-vous d'amoureux, auxquels nous courions furtivement, le coeur battant et la pensée frémissante" (p. 468). Coded letters left in a secret hiding-place and floral talismans of faithful love were manifestations of their affection. But Gide is careful to add: "Si passionnée que fût notre liaison, il ne s'y glissait de sensualité pas la moindre. Lionel, d'abord, était richement laid; puis sans doute éprouvais-je déjà cette inhabileté foncière à mêler l'esprit et les sens, qui je crois m'est assez particulière, et qui devait bientôt devenir une des répugnances cardinales de ma vie" (p. 469). This is the first explicit indication of the young *adolescent*'s possible interest in homosexual activity. At the same time this passage summarizes the principle of the separation of desire from love to which he would for the most part remain faithful throughout his adult life. Not only was Lionel's appearance an additional discouraging factor here; so was his heterosexuality. "Non; entre eux, les hommes ne s'embrassent pas!" he said to Gide, who wanted to give him a farewell kiss (p. 469).

The foreshadowing becomes increasingly explicit and tantalizing from this point on. In Chapter Seven, Gide admits the self-deceit that was involved in his attributing to virtue his lack of interest in the opposite sex and his revulsion when confronted by prostitutes: "Certains jours qu'il m'arrive de croire au diable, quand je pense à mes saintes révoltes, à mes nobles hérissements, il me semble entendre l'*autre* rire et se frotter les mains dans l'ombre. Mais pouvais-je pressentir quels lacs . . . ? Ce n'est pas le lieu d'en parler" (p. 486). The *points de suspension* create their desired effect. The reader's curiosity is aroused about the secret Gide is withholding. Suspension points occur again, casting an ominous shadow on the ecstasy he found in the austerity of

41

puritanism: "Mais pouvais-je déjà comprendre le sens de ce qui se dessinait en moi? ... " (p. 501). The puritanism is more clearly insidious in Chapter Nine: "Mon éducation puritaine avait fait un monstre des revendications de la chair; comment eussé-je compris, en ce temps, que ma nature se dérobait à la solution la plus généralement admise, autant que mon puritanisme la réprouvait?" (p. 522). The metaphor of the monster that the natural rights of the flesh had become, and the rhetorical question, make the reader aware of how tenuous and artificial Gide's excessive mental chastity really was. It was indeed most impermanent. In the midst of the literary personages introduced in Chapter Ten, suspension points hint at more revelations to come: "Au vrai, j'étais grisé par la diversité de la vie, qui commençait à m'apparaître, et par ma propre diversité. ... Mais je m'étais promis, dans ce chapitre de ne parler que du voisin. J'y reviens" (p. 543). Because of Gide's consistent but not excessive use of foreshadowing, the reader will be ready to accept the details of the sexual initiation in Part Two.

Foreshadowing is not the only device that Gide borrowed from fiction. Louis Aragon, on reading Gide's *Pages de Journal 1929-1932,* commented: "Ce livre capital, on peut le lire presque à la façon d'un roman."[2] He thought that he was paying Gide a compliment, and so he was. He could, moreover, have paid him the same compliment in reference to *Si le grain ne meurt.* The structure of Gide's autobiography can be, and in fact should be, studied in the same way as that of a first-person novel. In the first place, it almost satisfies the definition of a first-person novel: "By a first-person novel is meant a novel that is narrated all the way along in the first person by a person who appears in the novel, the narrator."[3] The narrator of *Si le grain ne meurt* is André Gide, who appears in the pivotal role of protagonist as well as narrator. André Gide, narrator, fails to fit into our definition only in so far as in fiction we expect that the protagonist-narrator's name will not be the same as the author's. We may *expect* this; however, we do not *require* it. We must remember that to all intents and purposes the given name of Marcel Proust's narrator in his long autobiographical *novel* is the same as the author's,[4] and conversely that the autobiography

---

2. In *L'Humanité,* le 25 juin 1934.

3. Bertil Romberg, *Studies in the Narrative Technique in the First-Person Novel* (Stockholm, 1962), p. 4. This work, along with Wayne C. Booth's *The Rhetoric of Fiction* (Chicago, 1961), are the most useful guides for structure study in first-person fiction.

4. Philippe Lejeune, for one, is unready to accept this traditional viewpoint. See "Le Pacte autobiographique", p. 149.

called the *Vie de Henry Brulard* is *really* the autobiography of one Henri Beyle. There seems, then, to be no fixed ruling that autobiographers' narrators retain their own names, or that novelists must change theirs. We may, consequently, consider the narrator of *Si le grain ne meurt* to be a *persona* of André Gide, in much the same way that we consider Henry Brulard to be a *persona* of Stendhal, or the poet of "Le Lac" to be a *persona* of Lamartine. André Gide's many-sided personality, his tendency to present only a portion of himself in each of his works, and his very specific purpose in writing *Si le grain ne meurt* invite us to say that the image of himself which Gide projects through his mode of narration is a selective one, and that certain sides of himself indeed have been masked, as the word *persona* suggests.

André Gide, narrator, then, is not to be confused with André Gide the man, who lived the life that is being described and analysed in the work. Nor is he to be confused with an intermediate entity, André Gide the author, who conceived the work and set the words on paper. André Gide the narrator is a creation of André Gide the author, a creation who sees the world in a way which André Gide the author has chosen for him. The voice which André Gide the narrator uses will also have been chosen for him. The material which will form his story will be the life of André Gide the man. One must also reckon with a fourth entity, André Gide the hero of the work. For we must be sceptical about accepting all the details of the life of André Gide the hero as the same as those of André Gide the man. Discrepancies in fact, magnification of incidental moments, omission of important events, must all be considered as not just possible but inevitable. And too many years have passed for the narrator to view all events in the same light as the young hero. We are, after all, witnessing in the story the evolution of this young hero. André Gide the hero, who seems to a reader to be an authentic recollection of André Gide the narrator, has actually been created (like the narrator) by André Gide the author. We are thus confronted with the following house-that-Jack-built situation: A man named André Gide lived a life which in his role as an author by the name of André Gide he has recreated in a book where a narrator (also named André Gide) tells the life of his younger self, the hero, who of course was also called André Gide. This reminds one of nothing so much as a certain man named Marcel Proust who was also an author whose narrator in a long first-person novel tells the story of himself (called Marcel) living and maturing with events and people surprisingly similar to those in the first Marcel Proust's life. It is easy to see that such a variation on the *style en abîme* would be pleasing to the author of *Les Faux-monnayeurs*.

At the risk of sounding simplistic, we repeat that *A la recherche du temps perdu* is a novel and *Si le grain ne meurt* an autobiography. But what Bertil Romberg would call the "epic-situation" of their narration is not dissimilar.[5] A middle-aged man is looking backward on his life and recording certain recollections. Both narrators have a field of vision as wide as their own experiences will allow, or in the case of events they did not witness, as far-reaching as their informants' knowledge can carry them. Following the example of Leo Spitzer, Romberg would call both narrators the "erzählendes Ich". This is the I who has already lived the experiences of the "erlebendes Ich", the I whose story is being traced in the narrative in the past. The time of Proust's epic-situation, revealed at the end of the novel, immediately follows the Princesse de Guermantes's reception at which the narrator supposedly receives the inspiration to write the book we are reading. In *Si le grain ne meurt* the time of the narration is less explicit. We must grasp at details such as references to *L'Immoraliste* (p. 561), *Amyntas* (p. 590), *La Porte étroite* (pp. 508,523), and *La Symphonie pastorale* (p. 553) as works with which Gide assumed his readers would be already familiar at the time of composition. If it were not for these references and a footnote on page 549 which indicates that the beginning of Part Two was being written in the spring of 1919, the epic-situation could be placed at almost any period between the time of the narrator-hero's engagement on the final page of the text (1895) and the date of publication (1920-1). While it would seem that the narrator probably concluded his story some time in 1919, there is still no textual clue as to the beginning of his *Erzählzeit* (i.e., the time when he is telling the story). One wishes for one of those cryptic dates of composition such as Montherlant obligingly gives us at the conclusion of *Les Célibataires* ("mai-août 1933"), or as Gide himself offers at the end of *Le Voyage d'Urien* ("La Roque. Eté 1892"). Gide's *erzählte Zeit,* or the length of time covered in the protagonist's evolution is, of course, quite clearly from November 1869 to the summer of 1895, with occasional references to earlier family history and more recent events.

The place of the epic-situation for this sort of narration is usually the aging narrator's writing-desk. If he does not tell us this, we automatically assume it. Gide's narrator tells us that his desk is at Cuverville (p. 358), and that at least once he leaves it to write in the garden (p. 411). For the purposes of his book, this conveys an aura of gracious country-living; and it is soon forgotten that sources other than the text (Gide's *Journal* and the notebooks of Mme van Rysselberghe) inform us that in fact Gide wrote his autobiography in a variety of places.

It is almost by necessity characteristic of first-person narrators that they should rely on verb tenses for establishing the distance between the *Erzählzeit* and the *erzählte Zeit*.[6] When Gide uses the present tense in the narration of *Si le grain ne meurt,* he is most often speaking of his epic-situation as the mature autobiographer. Inevitably a large number of present tenses appear in the first few pages as he leads the reader into his narration of the past. The words " je revois" occur, in fact, three times on the first page. Synonyms will be "je me souviens" or "je me rappelle" or "j'imagine".

Occasionally the deferential conditional serves as the equivalent of the present: "Je voudrais, pour parler de vous, inventer des mots plus vibrants, plus respectueux et plus tendres" (p. 363). Gide also sometimes uses the future and even the pluperfect subjunctive (replacing a conditional anterior) in his role as mature narrator: "Ceci donnera la mesure de son cynisme" (p. 587), and "Comment eût-il été question de travail?" (p. 436). These tenses add variety to the style of the narrative without diminishing the force of present time. The corresponding past tense is the past indefinite: "J'ai décrit de mon mieux cette sorte de suffocation profonde" (pp.484-5), or "En décrivant notre appartement, j'ai réservé la bibliothèque" (p. 486).

In this sort of prose, the use of the *passé indéfini* to refer to the recent past very clearly restores the original difference between it and the *passé défini*. The *passé défini* is used here as the principal tense for narration of the events that took place in the more distant past: "Je naquis le 22 novembre 1869" (p. 349). These stylistic habits can result in the following unusual but quite correct blending of tenses: "Je ne sais plus. J'ai exigé de moi cette promesse de ne point chercher à meubler les chambres vides du souvenir. Mais j'acceptai de sortir avec eux après dîner" (pp. 584-5).

For vividness, of course, past events are sometimes narrated in the *présent historique* instead of the *passé défini*. Gide allots this stylistic tribute to his very early recollection of a torchlight parade in Rouen (p. 360), the ball in the rue de Crosne (pp. 361-3), his schoolboy fights while at the Pension Vedel (p.

6. Jean Starobinski also mentions this characteristic of autobiography in "Le Style de l'autobiographie", *Poétique,* no. 3 (1970), pp. 257-65.

408), the illness feigned for the doctors and his Uncle Charles at Montpellier (p. 426), the almost disastrous reading of Gautier with his mother (p. 489), his first homosexual experience (p. 560), and the arrival of Mériem for his first heterosexual one (p. 566).

The subject of the narrator's thoughts in present time are usually his purpose in writing, comments on his faulty memory, the organization of his material, some guidelines concerning his structure, self-analysis, philosophical aphorisms, or descriptions of places as they still appear at the time of writing. Each of these subjects reveals some details of the narrator's character.

The narrator's comments on the purpose of writing depict him as devoted to honesty: "Je rougis à vous la redire — mais ce n'est pas un roman que j'écris et j'ai résolu de ne me flatter dans ces mémoires, non plus en surajoutant du plaisant qu'en dissimulant le pénible" (p. 369); and "mais ce n'est pas la vraisemblance que je poursuis, c'est la vérité" (p. 594). They also reveal him to be inconsistent. At the beginning of Part One he said: "Mettons que c'est par pénitence que je l'écris" (p. 349), but towards the end of Part Two when he is reconciling himself with his new hedonism, there is much less question of either self-judgement or penitence: "Le ton de ces dernières lignes va laisser croire que j'ai passé condamnation là-dessus; mais plutôt il y faudrait voir de la précaution, de la réponse à tout ce que je sais que l'on peut m'objecter; une façon de faire entendre que déjà je me l'objectais à moi-même; car je ne pense pas qu'il y ait façon d'envisager la question morale et religieuse, ni de se comporter en face d'elle, qu'à certain moment de ma vie je n'aie connue et faite mienne" (pp. 606-7). The author who had signed works under the general title of "Ne Jugez Pas", and who was to state the liberating purpose behind his autobiography elsewhere, could not, after all, speak otherwise. Can we not interpret the penitential narrator of the opening pages as a diplomatic ploy to prevent his less liberal-minded readers from rejecting his indiscretions too early?

A faulty memory will be by far the most frequent subject of commentary for André Gide the narrator. As often as he is able to say "je me souviens", he is called on to say: "je ne me souviens pas" (p. 352), "je ne me rappelle qu'une" (p. 356), "je ne sais plus à quelle occasion" (p. 368), "le seul dont il me souvienne" (p. 369), "je ne suis pas certain que" (p. 381), "mes souvenirs ternis" (p. 384), "si je ne fais erreur" (p. 386), etc. Just as much as the recurring "je me souviens" and its synonyms inspire confidence concerning the narrator's veracity, so do the negative forms. For who could trust a narrator who claimed to have a perfect memory? André Gide, the narrator of his life-story, becomes humanized, and one counts on him to distinguish between clear and hazy recollections. He does not disappoint us. We find, for instance, both "Je me souviens avec précision" (p. 384), and "je n'ai conservé d'elle qu'un souvenir indistinct" (p. 444). If his memory is not altogether clear, at least his integrity in telling us so is exceptional. With these passages Gide is able to arouse the reader's sympathy. It is not surprising that they become less necessary after the first few chapters, and accordingly less frequent. But they do not by any means disappear.

Gide's memory, apparently, had its greatest difficulty with dates: "Ma mémoire ne se trompe pas souvent de place; mais elle brouille les dates" (p. 360). The narrator tells us, therefore, that he will organize his recollections around places and people rather than chronologically. In point of fact, the chronological presentation is much more consistent than he promises on page 360, and the only notable backtracking he does is in Chapter Five when he must pick up some incidents that occurred before the move from the rue de Tournon to the rue de Commaille, and in Chapter Nine, where at the beginning he returns to the death of Anna Shackleton which had occurred several years earlier, and at the end introduces his "cousine de Feuchères" whom he could have mentioned as early as Chapter One.

We become involved with him in other problems of composition: his difficulty in describing places (p. 385), the retention or omission of some pages on Gérardmer (p. 429), the autobiographer's perpetual problem of being able to portray only the concrete and not the more elusive impressions, emotions, or sensations (pp. 492 and 500-1), and his general dissatisfaction with what he has written (p. 527).

Gide's fullest and most satisfying statement on the autobiographer's plight is found in the oft-quoted note which he appended to Part One. This is the note in which Gide uses Roger Martin du Gard's remarks about vagueness in the self-portrait in *Si le grain ne meurt* as a point of departure for a criticism of autobiography (or *mémoires*) in general.[7] He has been anxious to tell all, but cramped by the fact that excessive

---

7. Martin du Gard's conversation with Gide relevant to this note took place on October 6, 1920, according to the *Journal,* p. 683. A long and important letter from Martin du Gard dated October 7, 1920, clarifies his points of criticism. *Correspondance Gide-Martin du Gard,* I: 156-9.

confidences can seem unnatural, and naturalness is by all means to be sought. Moreover, since he is himself a creature of dialogue, he would like to be able to present both sides of his contradictory self simultaneously, a phenomenon which the genre does not allow. "Les Mémoires ne sont jamais qu'à demi sincères, si grand que soit le souci de vérité: tout est toujours plus compliqué qu'on ne le dit. Peut-être même approche-t-on de plus près la vérité dans le roman" (p. 547).[8]

Gide's narration keeps the reader constantly in mind. He seems to have realized that if he was going to take liberties with the chronological ordering of his past, he must make his reader aware of just where or when the events occurred, and sometimes why he is steering his narrative in the direction it is taking. The result is that the narration contains a good deal of scaffolding (forty examples in fact), just enough for most readers to be grateful without feeling that their intelligence is being belittled. These structural guidelines — usually brief — sometimes indicate the beginning of a digression: "Cette étrange aventure m'en persuade, qu'il faut que je raconte aussitôt, bien qu'elle soit de ma dix-huitième (?) année" (p. 373), or the return from one: "Mais je reviens à ma lecture de Gautier" (p. 489). They may explain that the narrator is still speaking of events in a certain setting: "Avant de quitter Uzès avec elle, je veux parler" (p. 383), or is moving on to a new subject: "Le moment est peut-être venu de m'expliquer là-dessus" (p. 525). Sometimes he refers back to earlier episodes: "J'ai dit déjà la vigilance de ma mère à ne m'avantager en rien sur d'autres camarades moins fortunés" (p. 473), or earlier omissions: "Entraîné par mon récit, je n'ai su parler en son temps de la mort d'Anna" (p. 507). Sometimes he promises later episodes: "La maison de mon oncle était aussi banale et maussade que la rue. J'en reparlerai plus tard" (p. 411). He does not always keep his promise, as in the case of his cousin Georges Pouchet, who, having been postponed for later discussion on page 415, is dismissed in a single sentence on page 551. Further mention of Maeterlinck, Marcel Schwob, and Barrès, promised on page 547, never appears.

Most often, the scaffolding serves as transition into the next episode. This is particularly true of chapter conclusions. Gide

8. This note has already been discussed in Chapter I, *supra*. Lejeune adds still further light to the matter by seeing in the note an *extension* of the autobiographical pact to include Gide's novels. Gide is subtly using his note to attract attention to the autobiographical aspects of his fiction. See Lejeune, "Le Pacte autobiographique", pp. 158-60.

tantalizes the reader at the end of Chapter Two with: "C'est peu de temps ensuite que je fus renvoyé de l'Ecole, pour des motifs tout différents que je vais tâcher d'oser dire" (p. 390). Chapter Three concludes: "Le bonheur de les revoir l'emportait presque, ou tout à fait, sur mon chagrin. Il est temps que je parle d'elles" (p. 410). His comments here on the cousins whom he is going to discuss in the following chapter are brief and urgent enough to make the reader read right on. Gide has simply used an old but trustworthy technique of story-telling, which detective-story writers have used with consistent success. My analogy with the *roman policier* is not meant to be derogatory to either that worthy genre or Gide's autobiography. Gide, who would later read Georges Simenon with pleasure, had already learned the tricks of suspense writing.

The narrator's direct self-analysis is spasmodic and limited. For the most part he lets the episodes speak for themselves as far as revelations about the young Gide are concerned. Like Montaigne, like his own Michel in *L'Immoraliste,* he describes the self without excessive analysis or judgement. When the self-commentary *does* occur, it tends to be in the first part consistently unkind. Of himself at a *very* early age, the narrator says: "A cet âge innocent où l'on voudrait que toute l'âme ne soit que transparence, tendresse et pureté, je ne revois en moi qu'ombre, laideur, sournoiserie" (pp. 349-50). A little older, he will be "le petit ignorant que j'étais" (p. 387), and at the Ecole Alsacienne: "Je le répète: je dormais encore; j'étais pareil à ce qui n'est pas encore né" (p. 390). The direct self-criticism becomes less frequent after the first two chapters. The reader watches the young boy vegetate through several chapters of mediocre school- and piano-teachers until he blossoms forth under the guidance of Messrs. Keller, Simonnet, Dietz, and de la Nux. Throughout these chapters (Three to Nine), the commentary tends to treat truths about the mature Gide which he feels also applied to him as a child and help explain his actions then. Under this pretext he is able to tell us that he has never loved the theatre (p. 466); he has always been by nature obedient (p. 487); he has had little aptitude for historical studies (pp. 488-9); he finds it difficult to conceal his joy (p. 494); he is masochistic enough to take pleasure in failure (p. 524); and likes honest compliments while detesting awkward flattery (p. 526). The longest portion of self-analysis pertains to his patient resignation in the face of years of commercially and critically unsuccessful writing (pp. 524-7).

In Part Two the self-analysis in the present quite expectedly relates most often to the question of Gide's sexual liberation, and he is again careful to analyse his feelings and actions as they were in the 1890s. He stresses the firmness of the resolution to experience sexual encounters which lay behind his 1893 trip to Africa (pp. 552, 564), his sense of optimistic fatalism (p. 559), the curiosity which caused his hesitancy in yielding to Ali (p. 561), his conscious cruelty in explaining his relationship with Mériem to his mother (p. 569), the joy he felt in conversations with Paul Laurens (p. 571), his distaste for Laurens's beautiful mistress (p. 572), etc. The fact that all these emotions are introduced by a "je crois que" or an "il me souvient que" in the present tense not only lends immediacy to the narrative but also reminds the reader that his narrator's intelligence and memory are actively involved in recreating as accurate an impression as possible of emotions which are long past and which may not have been fully understood at the time. It has taken several hundred pages for the narrator to feel that he has inspired the confidence necessary for a sympathetic acceptance of his revelations. In these crucial chapters the present tense subtly brings the reader into close contact with the now familiar narrator, while at the same time rendering the past events even more distant. The reader is, then, ready to respond to the middle-aged narrator's request for understanding, without feeling obliged to share the young man's passion in Africa: "Au nom de quel Dieu, de quel idéal me défendez-vous de vivre selon ma nature? Et cette nature, où m'entraînerait-elle, si simplement je la suivais?" (p. 550).

In the sections of narrator's commentary, the phrasing of certain sentences results in the formation of philosophical aphorisms important to the intellectual authority of the narrative presence. These sentences could be anthologized, and indeed some have been. They provide a varied range of Gidean views:

"Toute chose appartient à qui sait en jouir" (p. 393);

"La sympathie peut faire éclore bien des qualités somnolentes" (p. 400);

"Hélas! pour qui connut le dieu, combien mornes et désespérées les périodes débilitées où il ne consent plus à paraître!" (p. 485);

"Les traits les plus marquants d'un caractère se forment et s'accusent avant qu'on en ait pris conscience" (p. 501);

"Le motif secret de nos actes, et j'entends: des plus décisifs, nous échappe; et non seulement dans le souvenir que nous en gardons, mais bien au moment même" (p. 561);

"Il est des êtres qui s'éprennent de ce qui leur ressemble;
d'autres de ce qui diffère d'eux" (p. 565);

"Nos actes les plus sincères sont aussi les moins calculés;
l'explication qu'on en cherche après coup reste vaine" (p. 613).

As a group, these sentences share a fundamental interest in mankind's joys and sorrows, his unity and diversity, expressed in a classically economical form. They seem to be the words of a man who has learned his philosophy from Montaigne, his phrasing from La Rochefoucauld. They thus contribute to an honest portrait of their author.

The places and objects described in the present tense take on a permanence which links their related events not only to the time of narration but even to the time of reading the work. Kaleidoscopes, Anna Shackleton's water-colours, La Fontaine d'Eure, and the lake at Neuchâtel are in fact still with us; and if the water-colours have faded or progress has changed the face of the terrain at Neuchâtel, the ravages of time have been infinitely less severe on them than on the people with whom they were associated in Gide's life and narrative. While less obsessed with the theme of time than Marcel Proust, Gide was no less sensitive to the effect of verb tenses on the sense of time conveyed by his prose. In this case, it is the durative quality of the present tense which he has exploited.

The bulk of *Si le grain ne meurt* consists, then, of a combination of narration in the past and, to a lesser extent, commentary in the present. We shall call these two modes of narration the primary narrative techniques of the work. The narrator is well aware of the more stimulating value of unanalysed narration, and must occasionally curb his desire to comment: "Mais je réserve les commentaires et reviens à mes souvenirs" (p. 466). Within these two primary narrative techniques, one finds a variety of secondary techniques. We have already referred to the aphorisms and descriptions within the commentary, and there are even more descriptions within the narration in the past. The descriptions of La Roque (pp. 394-5) and of Uzès (pp. 369-70) have for a long time been considered purple passages. There are too many to enumerate. Their purpose is clearly to provide a point of contrast between the long years of childhood in the almost cloistered Norman countryside and the exciting voyages of early manhood to the sunny and free North African oases. The descriptions of Part One are particularly useful for slowing down the narrative. In Part Two Gide confesses that he has

described Kairouan and events there only to hold off the encounter with the young Arab, Ali: "Pourquoi je raconte tout
cela? Oh! simplement pour retarder ce qui va suivre. Je sais que
cela n'a pas d'intérêt" (p. 559).

Scenes of dialogue also slow down the narrative. There are
proportionately more of these in Part One than in Part Two, but
they are not noticeably frequent anywhere. A study of the
manuscript and of subsequent variants reveals that direct discourse gave Gide considerable difficulty. Both for this reason,
and because conversations recalled verbatim by a narrator many
years after they take place require from the reader a suspension of
disbelief, it is surprising that Gide has used direct discourse
even as much as he has. It would appear that his artistic desire to
vary the narrative technique occasionally triumphed over the
difficulty of composition and the peril to *vraisemblance*.

The interior monologue remembered verbatim also takes for
granted the reader's co-operation in suspending disbelief. Gide
uses this technique only about a dozen times within his narrative in the past. Some of these examples are introduced by a verb
of saying or thinking: "Quoi! ce n'est là, me redisais-je, qu'une
famille de paysans! quelle élégance, quelle vivacité, quelle
noblesse, auprès de nos épais cultivateurs de Normandie!" (p.
374), or, "Oh! me disais-je, imiter ce qu'on imagine!" (p. 424).
Others are in the form of *discours indirect libre:* "J'éprouvais avec
lui le même désenchantement qu'avec M. Couve lors de mon
instruction religieuse. Quoi! c'était là cette science suprême
dont j'espérais l'éclaircissement de ma vie, ce sommet de la
connaissance d'où l'on pût contempler l'univers . . . Je me
consolais avec Schopenhauer" (p. 518). Here, the imperfect
tenses, indicative and subjunctive, have been transposed from
the present of the narrator's original mental articulation. The
same is true of the following example: "Certainement j'étais
heureux de la revoir, et de lui montrer ce pays; n'empêche que
nous étions consternés: notre vie commune commençait de si
bien s'arranger; cette rééducation de nos instincts, à peine
entreprise, allait-il falloir l'interrompre?" (p. 568). In this
example, however, the part after the colon, the free indirect
speech, may have been originally either the coincidental
thoughts of Laurens and Gide or part of a dialogue.[9] In general,

---

9. Gide also sometimes uses *discours indirect libre* to report direct dialogue,
or, as in the following example, the contents of letters: "Quelles lettres je
reçus! Supplications, objurgations, menaces; en ramenant Athman à
Paris, je me couvrirais de ridicule; que ferais-je de lui? Que penserait de
moi Emmanuèle?. . ." (p. 602).

the infrequency of this technique, as unobtrusive as it is, would seem to be caused by Gide's concern for *vraisemblance*.

While writing *Si le grain ne meurt,* Gide often complained that his style was too studied, subtle, dry, elegant, soporific, precious, or rhythmic — in short, too literary.[10] The manuscript's many corrections and hesitations show quite clearly that Gide indeed expended much energy in hunting for the elusive *mot juste*. One result of this is that several descriptive passages are masterpieces of form and diction. Their appeal is, however, intellectual rather than emotional. There is very little danger of calling them lyrical. This is not true of certain other passages, so few in number and so strikingly different in tone that we might even call them epiphanies. They are characterised by rhythmic syntax and rhetorical flair, which, while present in individual sentences throughout the whole work, never capture our attention so much as when consistent throughout a whole paragraph. The principal epiphanies or privileged moments in the narrative are: the descriptions of Anna Shackleton (pp. 363-4), of the boy at the costume-ball (pp. 406-7), of the flora at the Ile Sainte-Marguerite near Cannes (p. 436); an evocation of Emmanuèle (p. 453), of Anton Rubinstein (p. 465), of games at Val-Richer (p. 467); the joys of asceticism (p. 500); the first view of Tunis (pp. 554-5); an ecstatic awareness of convalescence (p. 570); an evening with Athman's brother (p. 603); and the sense of liberation at the death of Madame Paul Gide (p. 612).

A brief analysis of one of these passages — on Rubinstein — should serve to show what we mean by Gide's lyricism:

> Son prestige était considérable. Il ressemblait à Beethoven, de qui certains le disaient fils (je n'ai pas été vérifier si son âge rendait cette supposition vraisemblable); visage plat aux pommettes marquées, large front à demi noyé dans une crinière abondante, sourcils broussailleux; un regard absent ou dominateur; la mâchoire volontaire, et je ne sais quoi de hargneux dans l'expression de la bouche lippue. Il ne charmait point, il domptait. L'air hagard, il paraissait ivre, et l'on disait que souvent il l'était. Il jouait les yeux clos et comme ignorant du public. Il ne semblait point tant présenter un morceau que le chercher, le découvrir, ou le composer à mesure, et non point dans une improvisation, mais dans une ardente vision

---

10. See *Journal,* le 13 octobre, le 17 décembre, le 23 décembre 1916; le 23 septembre 1917; le 7 janvier 1918; le 1er novembre 1920 (pp. 572, 584, 586, 632, 643-4, 685).

intérieure, une progressive révélation dont lui-même éprouvât et ravissement et surprise.

This is a passage which maintains a suggestive balance between the distinction of the artist as the adult world could appreciate him, and the extraordinary impression he could make on a marvelling, sensitive child. It builds from its first short general sentence to the more complex description of Rubinstein's physical appearance. In this sentence the possible kinship with Beethoven, of interest to the adult world ("de qui certains le disaient fils"), is dismissed as less important than the fact that he *resembled* Beethoven. Gide's parenthesis is, after all, a rhetorical *dubitatio,* and even at the age of writing he has not verified if the kinship could be true. The important words here are the substantives. First come the ternary "visage", "front", and "sourcils" accompanied by their modifiers, each phrase apparently building in length, but instead dramatically ending on the brief minor cadence, "sourcils broussailleux". The lack of co-ordinating connectives (asyndeton) makes the reader rely on the vocal accentuation of the substantives, and the style approaches the classical *style nominal.* We move from the craggy upper face to its expression, with the antithetical adjectives "absent ou dominateur". This phrase is given special significance by being isolated from the surrounding part of the sentence by a pair of semicolons. It is followed by the description of the lower portion of the face with its strong jaw and full, sulky lips. The expression "je ne sais quoi" suggests that the young boy's reaction to the pianist's appearance has been non-analytical, and reminds us that it is his point of view we are sharing. The following sentence provides a balanced and brief rhetorical leap from negation of his ability to charm to affirmation of his power to conquer. This is a pure example of the *correctio* in Roman rhetoric. In the next sentence, which considers both his illusion of inebriation and the possible reality that this was his actual state, the two-part balance is maintained almost down to the number of syllables in each part. The next two sentences, both beginning with "il", emphasize the genius of the performer. The anaphora, though undistinguished, does serve to keep the pianist centre-stage in the narrative. The first of these two sentences repeats the concision of the two preceding sentences, but it is the second, longer one which interests us more. It soon returns to the ternary rhythm found in the earlier nouns, and though this time Gide uses three verbs, "chercher", "découvrir", and "composer", to stress the personal quality of Rubinstein's interpretation, it is the infinitive form he chooses, the verb form most closely linked to the noun. We have here, then, an echo of the only other long sentence in the paragraph. This time he does not omit the connectives. Instead we find a total of five co-ordinating conjunctions which help this sentence to flow to its climax. The earlier *correctio* is also echoed in the "non point dans . . . mais dans" construction, and we are made more fully aware of the special quality of the pianist's inspiration by the placing of the adjectives "ardente" and "progressive" before their substantives "vision" and "révélation". Finally, these two nouns acquire an indefinite quality from the use of the subjunctive mood for "éprouvât" in their dependent subordinate clause. While an indicative would have been correct, it would have suggested less well the astonishment Rubinstein himself apparently felt on almost mystically discovering his interpretation. The climax of the sentence, the double-barrelled "ravissement et surprise", is grammatically Rubinstein's, but the structure of the paragraph is such that the reader knows that the delight and surprise are certainly the young Gide's as well. The controlled accumulation of various rhetorical effects has been blended in the long final sentence to recreate his enchantment at the concert. The young Gide who felt these reactions could not have described them this effectively. It has taken the mature author to give them lyrical expression.

Apart from the obvious pivotal comparison of Rubinstein with Beethoven, analogies and images are of minor importance to the lyricism of the passage. The comparison of a forehead with a half-drowned body in "front à demi noyé" may be eye-catching, but the analogy between shaggy hair and a horse's mane in "crinière" and the comparison of eyebrows with underbrush in "sourcils broussailleux" are common enough to be hardly worth noting. Gide has instead relied on syntax and rhetoric to create his emotional effect. This is true of most of *Si le grain ne meurt*; for while occasionally he falls back on the ejaculatory style of *Les Nourritures terrestres*, the greater part of the work is written without reliance on exclamations, vocatives, or even analogous imagery.[11] The most recurrent device he uses instead is that of ternary rhythm. One can count more than a hundred obvious examples of the device, roughly one in every two and a half Pléiade pages of text. The technique is used for all kinds of occasions — from a description of little Mouton, "délicat, doux, tranquille" (p. 352), to the marble in the wall at

---

11. For exceptions, however, see the exclamations on pages 467, 497, 500, 554, 570, and 603.

Uzès, "quelque chose de rond, de gris, de lisse" (p. 383), or to the tone of Lord Alfred Douglas's voice: "sifflante, méprisante, haineuse" (p. 586). As the undisputed stylistic dominant, it contributes highly to the work's texture of classical dignity. In Part Two, where the lyrical passages also become proportionately more frequent, the ternary practice is, however, almost outdistanced by enumerations: "Timidité, pudeur, dégoût, fierté, sentimentalité mal comprise, effarouchement nerveux à la suite d'une maladroite expérience (c'était le cas de Paul, je crois) tout cela retient sur le seuil" (p. 552); and "Il y eut, dans une petite mosquée, une séance d'aïssaouas, qui dépassa en frénésie, en étrangeté, en beauté, en noblesse, en horreur, tout ce que je pus voir ensuite" (p. 559). The frequent addition of this device dear to the heart of Victor Hugo may to some extent account for the "romantic" effect of many of the exotic pages in Part Two.

Admirers of *Paludes* and *Les Caves du Vatican* will have appreciated yet another stylistic aspect of *Si le grain ne meurt*: the occasional use of irony in the narrative voice. There is understated self-mockery, for instance, in the narrator's observation after M. Richard (in real life M. Bauer) had killed Gide's friendly mice: "Et c'est moi qui les avais livrées! Décidément j'aurais dû lui demander d'abord s'il aimait les animaux . . ." (pp. 445-6). Shortly after, to avenge what he has considered injustice at the hands of Mme Bertrand (Garnier), the young boy self-righteously abstains from visiting his turtle-doves for two weeks. He expresses the ironically unexpected effect of his gesture in a forcefully brief sentence: "Le résultat fut excellent pour le travail" (p. 449). There is a wry touch in the unexpectedness of the final clause of a sentence about Ferdinand Hérold: "On le retrouvait chaque fois qu'on avait besoin de lui, et même plus souvent encore" (p. 540). And the conclusion to the fiasco with En Barka is a masterpiece of ironical circumlocution: "Je restai muet, et la quittai n'ayant pu lui donner que de l'argent" (p. 570).

The flashes of irony of expression are rare, however, and like lyricism stand out in contrast with the controlled rhetoric which generally characterizes the style. The narrative tone, as a result, is primarily serious and absorbing. One is led to question whether we were not premature in speaking earlier of the narrator of *Si le grain ne meurt* as yet another *persona* of the author of *Les Faux-monnayeurs*. Is this not the *natural* voice of André Gide himself, and for once do we not have man-author-narrator combined in one entity? I think not. In the first place, the narrative tone is, as Gide pointed out himself, too literary to be natural. And in the second place, Gide speaks sufficiently about his dissatisfaction with *this* style, which he proposes abandoning for another, that we feel obliged to say that it is just *one* of his many possible poses. Not unlike Rubinstein at the keyboard in the passage analysed above, Gide at his desk seemed never to know what style would be bestowed upon him for a certain work until he took pen in hand.[12]

12. W. M. Frohock in *Style and Temper* (Oxford, 1967), p. 10, quite rightly points out that the more serious narrating *persona* of *Les Faux-monnayeurs* seems to be more genuinely like Gide than the narrator of *Les Caves du Vatican*. Neither one is, however, the true André Gide, whose authentic voice cannot be found unreservedly even in his correspondence, which sometimes too strictly follows the formulas of the epistolary *bienséances*. Is it, after all, possible to speak of a single "natural" or "authentic" style in an author who wrote even his diary with a view to publication? Perhaps it is wisest to say that *all* of Gide's various voices are in their individual ways "authentic".

4

The Truth of an Autobiography

T HE structure of an autobiography can be analysed with the same tools as fiction. The autobiographer's obligation to a truthful self-representation, however, presents a problem which we do not find in fiction, where the freedom for fantasy is infinite. While it is true that an autobiographer is permitted inaccuracies in his details as well as *some* imaginative writing, it is also true that some doubts can be cast on the veracity of his total self-portrayal if much falsehood can be detected in even seemingly insignificant episodes. On the basis of both structure and fictionalization, Rousseau's *Confessions,* for instance, may indeed be the best French *novel* of the eighteenth century.[1]

Perhaps because it has been sometimes too lavishly praised, André Gide's famous "sincerity" has been at times called into question. Jacques Brenner has suggested that Gide's claim (in the *Journal*) to having read Radiguet's *Le Bal du comte d'Orgel* in 1924 was false.[2] In actual fact, says Brenner, in 1924 Gide was annoyed with all the publicity organized around this novel's publication, and quoted some of Bernard Faÿ's adverse criticism. When in 1933 Gide actually got around to reading the Radiguet work, he liked it. The most celebrated case of Gide's questionable reporting was the "Victor" incident. The young

---

1. The debate on accuracy of detail in the *Confessions* may never be totally resolved.
2. In "Le Péché d'inexactitude", *Cahiers des Saisons,* no. 17 (été 1959), pp. 163-5.

58

boy whom Gide discussed with a mixture of distaste and indiscretion (*Journal*, winter of 1942-3) attempted to challenge some of the attack under the pseudonym of François Derais.[3] The same Henri Rambaud who assisted "Victor" in this dispute has more recently raised another lively controversy over the accuracy of Gide's reporting of a famous statement of Madeleine Gide's in reference to her husband's attentiveness to some young boys on a train.[4] Perhaps the champion of all French sticklers for truth is Henri Guillemin. Gide's accuracy came up for scrutiny in Guillemin's first volume of truth-detection, *A vrai dire*.[5] He found pure fabrication in Gide's claim in the preface to the 1946 edition of *Pages de Journal 1939-1942* that he had made no changes since the original publication in *L'Arche*. Guillemin found many variants, including some important ones in two extracts that had been published in the collaborationist *Nouvelle Revue Française* for December 1940 and February 1941, an edition Gide omits from the work's bibliographical history in the 1946 preface. Gide's subsequent versions, said Guillemin, had been tidied up to sound more patriotic.[6] Doubtless there are further cases — each more trivial than the other — of doubting Gide's truthfulness. It is not our job to catalogue them here. Nor is it our intention to undertake the well-nigh impossible task of passing judgement on them. Suffice it to say that over the years not everyone has trusted Gide's veracity.

Much of the effectiveness of an autobiography depends on the author's factual dependability. Even if a reader admires the style or enjoys the anecdotes, he must still respect the truth of the work for it to be successful *as an autobiography*. Our few examples from other sources could be sufficient to make some readers sceptical about the reliability of the author of *Si le grain ne meurt*. But the final proof of Gide as a dependable autobiographer must lie in the capacity of the autobiography itself to pass the truth test, independent of factual discrepancies in other works. The

3. François Derais et Henri Rambaud, *L'Envers du "Journal" de Gide* (Paris, 1952).
4. Henri Rambaud, "La Phrase de Madeleine" in *Les Cahiers André Gide*, 1 (Paris, 1969), pp. 319-70. In both this article and his essay in *L'Envers du "Journal" de Gide*, Rambaud, who was an admirer of Gide's works, seems to believe that while Gide's sexual propensities caused him to alter details, an alert reader can still find the essential truth within the texts.
5. Henri Guillemin, "A propos du *Journal* d'André Gide", in *A vrai dire* (Paris, 1956), pp. 211-13.
6. A defendant for Gide's side emerged in the unlikely person of Henri Massis. See the *Bulletin des Lettres*, no. 155 (le 15 février 1954), pp. 56-63.

need to establish Gide's relative truthfulness in this single work has won out over Jean Collignon's discouraging but correct observation: "No pastime is more appealing to unemployed critics than collecting instances of contradiction in André Gide's words. This is a game where one scores at every other page; and a safe one, at that, for the opponent not only puts up no fight whatsoever, but also invites continuous attack."[7] Collignon is referring to Gide's contradiction in attitudes or ideas. Our search will be directed more basically and therefore all the more significantly towards contradictions between the truth of reality and the fiction which can evolve through the two stages of personal recollection and literary transposition necessarily experienced by every autobiographer. Among the many factors causing errors will be the two *bêtes noires* of Marcel Proust, the insufficiency of voluntary memory, and an overactive imagination.

It is Jean Delay who is most helpful in recording some of Gide's inconsistencies. He reminds us that Gide's ancestor, Marin Rondeaux, was historically less glamorous and more bourgeois than Gide describes him in his notes for *Si le grain ne meurt*.[8] These notes on his mother's ancestors were dictated to him by his aunt, Mme Henri Rondeaux, and any inaccuracies in this account might be attributed to her. Charles Rondeaux, for instance, was mayor of Rouen in 1792, and not in 1789 as Gide states. According to Delay, both Madame Rondeaux and André Gide spelled Gide's great-grandmother's name correctly at the time of dictation: Anne-Marie Dufou.[9] Since it is only with his own generation that Gide begins changing his relatives' names, it is inexplicable why this lady's name appears as "Dufour" in all editions of his text.

A letter from Gide's cousin, Maurice Démarest, corrects Gide's assumption that Anna Shackleton entered the Rondeaux home on the advice of Le Pasteur Roberty. She was, rather, introduced by other friends, the Rowcliffes. Moreover, contrary to what Gide seemed to think, his aunt Claire, Maurice Démarest's mother, had already been married for possibly ten years. More important than what is in the letter, though, is what Gide did with it. In an honourable display of devotion to truth, he appended it right away to the eighth chapter of the private edition which was about to go to press. And since then it has appeared at the end of Part Two in all editions. However,

---

7. Jean Collignon, "Gide's Sincerity", *Yale French Studies,* no. 7 (1951), p. 44.
8. Delay, *La Jeunesse d'André Gide,* I: 37.
9. *Ibid.*, p. 39.

the version found in the present editions is not the same as that
of its first printing! The variations are intriguing. The letter in
the private edition begins with a quite different paragraph:

> Nos arrière grands-pères Rondeaux de Sétry et Rondeaux de
> Monbray n'étaient pas, comme tu le dis, conseillers au
> Parlement de Normandie, mais à la Cour des Comptes et
> Aides, dont le bel hôtel existe encore sur la place Notre-Dame,
> en face de la cathédrale.

It continues with the second paragraph of the postscript of the
present edition before beginning the letter as we have it now.
The postscript of the private edition reads as follows:

> P.-Sc. Renseignements pris, M. Rondeaux de Monbray n'a
> jamais été industriel et il n'avait pas à refaire sa fortune qu'il
> avait conservée pendant la Révolution.
> Es-tu sûr que ce soit en 1789 qu'il ait été maire de Rouen et
> non plus tard?

Equally important are the changes Gide made in his own
introduction to the letter. In the original, he acknowledged that
M. Démarest's corrections were "importantes". He also explained that he was unable to incorporate them in the text of the
book, since the relevant pages had already gone to press. The
tone of the sentence is such as to suggest that in later editions
these mistakes might still be remedied: "Cependant l'on
avait commencé d'imprimer le livre et les premiers chapitres
étaient déjà tirés; il n'était plus temps d'apporter à mon texte
même les corrections qu'il eût fallu." In later editions, however,
both this sentence and the adjective "importantes" disappear.
Either Gide had decided that the corrections were in fact not
important enough to involve changes to his text, or else he felt
that the appended letter filled the bill. The latter supposition
may have been well grounded; but what are we to think of his
deliberately changing another person's letter which he is
theoretically presenting in the interests of accurate documentation? We may say that Gide was only acting like Henry James,
who, when accused of taking similar liberties with the text of
his brother William's correspondence, explained: "I daresay I
did instinctively regard it at the last as all *my* truth to do what I
would with."[10] Gide also could have found precedents for his
editorial changes in the practices of publishers of letters in the

10. Quoted by Roy Pascal in "The Autobiographical Novel and the
    Autobiography", *Essays in Criticism* IX (April 1959): 148.

seventeenth century.[11] But no matter how we try to explain Gide's emendations, very few readers will find them excusable.

It is generally agreed that André Gide was unjust to his father's relatives in *Si le grain ne meurt*. It is not verifiable that his father's three brothers who died before the age of one year were poorly cared for. Nor was it true that his grandfather refused all medical assistance for himself. He even allowed his health to be placed in the care of charlatans in his later years. Moreover, this same Tancrède Gide was a gentler person than Gide allowed.[12] The stern portrait of his Uncle Charles Gide is similarly unjust. The recent disclosure of two handwritten pages which Gide withheld from the published versions of *Si le grain ne meurt* supports Delay's theory that the austerity of Charles Gide was meant by contrast to emphasize the warmth of personality of Gide's father. These pages containing two versions of an incident from Charles Gide's childhood throw a more human light on the economist.[13] We see him as a young boy restless to join in the noonday games of some of the barefoot boys of Uzès with whom he usually did not associate. This incident would have been totally out of keeping with the usual cool and self-assured portrait which André Gide created for his uncle in *Si le grain ne meurt*.

Gide's literary treatment of his parents is also misleading. His father was not so gentle a person as Gide presents him. Delay informs us that when Paul Gide yielded to his wife's direction of their son's upbringing, he was merely typical of contemplative intellectuals who prefer not to create scenes with less intelligent but more stubborn adversaries.[14] Nor was André Gide's mother the dragon she seems to be on a rapid reading of the text.[15] Gide later regretted the grimness of her portrait, and was happy to be able to retouch it in *Les Feuillets d'automne*. A closer reading of *Si le grain* itself shows her to be well-meaning and courageous.[16] We must not forget that at great risk to her

11. See Roger Duchêne, "Réalité vécue et réussite littéraire: Le Statut particulier de la lettre", *Revue d'Histoire Littéraire de la France*, 71e année, no. 2 (mars-avril 1971), pp. 177-94.

12. Delay, *La Jeunesse d'André Gide*, I: 57, 60.

13. Reported in the *Bulletin d'information de l'Association des Amis d'André Gide*, no. 5, le 15 octobre 1969, p. 3. First printed as "Une page inédite de *Si le grain ne meurt*", *Le Républicain d'Uzès et du Gard*, le 19 juillet 1969, pp. 1-2.

14. Delay, I: 79.

15. *Ibid.*, p. 81.

16. Pierre de Boisdeffre, *Vie d'André Gide 1869-1951: Essai de biographie critique*, vol. I, p. 42, reminds us that many of the qualities Gide found annoying in his mother would later characterize himself, qualities such as courage, stubbornness, and faith in a cause!

own health, Madame Paul Gide made a trip from Paris to La Roque to look after the farmers who were sick with typhoid fever. The contrast between the portraits of the two parents plays a part in the image of contrasting family origins which Gide chose to perpetuate; and by exaggerating his mother's portrait he successfully emphasized certain unfortunate aspects of the childhood environment from which he eventually escaped.

The effort to make his childhood seem cloistered extended to other inaccurate family images. Gide's uncle, Henri Rondeaux, was, for instance, far less colourless than Gide labels him. The same strength of character which permitted him at the age of twenty-five to convert to Catholicism in the midst of the most devout of Protestant households helped make him a firm and prosperous businessman.[17]

It would appear too that Gide was not altogether honest in his reporting of his youthful sex-life. Surely his activities with the *concierge*'s son, meant to orient readers on the first page, were more than sexual. Boisdeffre emphasizes that Gide omitted mention of his attempts to abstain from masturbation, a confession that would have harmed the sexual self-indulgence which we are meant to see as a natural instinct throughout his whole portrayal.[18] Furthermore, at the age of sixteen he was not so indifferent to the opposite sex as he claimed. Neither the pleasure of his explorations into seamy apartments with M. Richard, nor his violent reaction to prostitutes can be accurately considered as indifference.[19] In *Et nunc manet in te* he in fact admits that during summer vacations as a child he had indulged in sexual explorations with little girls, but not with little boys.[20]

It is Gide's self-confessed faulty sense of chronology which can be blamed for his mistake in dating the 1878 ball that he witnessed from the stairway in the rue de Crosne.[21] Equally excusable is another mistake; for nobody but a medical man such as Jean Delay himself would be able to detect Gide's error in calling a "percussion" an "auscultation" in relation to a consultation at Hyères (p. 435).[22]

There are a number of omissions from the text of characters or events that we might consider important in Gide's life-story.

17. Delay, I: 111.
18. Boisdeffre, *Vie d'André Gide,* I: 94-5.
19. Delay, I: 357-8.
20. *Et nunc manet in te,* p. 1131.
21. Delay, I: 147.
22. *Ibid.,* p. 303.

He could have said much more about his relationship with Lionel de R. (François de Witt). He kept notes in his unpublished Cahier d'Alençon which more explicitly show us how influential this friendship was; however, Gide could quite rightly feel justified in limiting his discussion of the family at Val-Richer to the rather full account which he has in fact left us.[23] The major aspects of the relationship are, after all, clearly recorded. More surprising is the omission of any mention at all of Le Pasteur Allégret who visited La Roque for several summers from 1885 on, and whose missionary experience in the Congo and pious teachings at La Roque would have had telling effects on André Gide.[24] Less surprising is his omission of the fact that Pierre Louÿs read to him the *Second Faust,* an event which marked him for life;[25] Gide tended generally to omit mention of the reading that contributed to his liberation, thus attributing all the more significance to people, places, and events. Art may have profited from the omission of what could have resulted in long digressions of literary criticism, but our honest understanding of the full scope of influences in the young Gide's life suffers. Delay finds great importance in an event which Gide has omitted from the account of his walking trip in Brittany. When the coachman of a carriage in which Gide was riding fell from his seat, Gide was obliged to take hold of the reins. He did so coolly, feeling strangely removed from a scene in which he was the principal participant. He later told Delay: "C'est ce jour-là que j'ai découvert l'ironie."[26] The three-month emancipating trip to Munich in the spring of 1892 is totally overlooked in *Si le grain ne meurt,*[27] perhaps because its existence would have taken some of the impact away from the African voyages. In the account of these latter voyages, he has omitted the copious and detailed notes which he kept about each of the Arab boys and which Delay has obligingly quoted.[28] The sharpness of Gide's portraits and the variety of the models make for interesting

23. *Ibid.,* p. 340.
24. *Ibid.,* p. 349. Gide maintained close relations with the Allégret family throughout his life.
25. *Ibid.,* p. 391.
26. *Ibid.,* p. 421. In a much modified form this incident found its way into *L'Immoraliste* as an event which acted as a catalyst to the consummation of Michel's and Marceline's marriage (pp. 404-5). Michel's punishment of the coachman in *L'Immoraliste* involves violence which is reminiscent of young Gide's treatment of the bully in the Pension Vedel (*Si le grain ne meurt,* p. 409).
27. See Delay, *La Jeunesse d'André Gide,* II: 152.
28. *Ibid.,* pp. 308-11.

reading, but perhaps the writer was afraid of satiating the readers of *Si le grain ne meurt* with such descriptions. Besides, he had already made use of some of this material in *L'Immoraliste*.

There are still other questionable statements. The father of Pierre Louÿs was not yet dead when the two boys became friends, although Gide suggests that Louÿs had already lost both parents (p. 505).[29] Alain Goulet has written on the second and third stanzas of Gide's poem "Solitude", only one stanza of which is quoted in *Si le grain ne meurt*. In the autobiography the poem takes on the role of an exercise which he was obliged to produce in fulfilment of his hasty promise to show Louÿs some of his verse. According to Goulet, the poem would seem, rather, to have been inspired by Gide's feelings for Louÿs, and the two missing stanzas, extant in the manuscript of *Nous deux*, do not conceal the warmth of his affection or the frustration at Louÿs's earlier cool response.[30]

Notes in Gide's agenda for early January 1891 reveal that Madeleine Rondeaux was more articulate about her opinion of *Les Cahiers d'André Walter* than he suggests Emmanuèle was on pages 529 and 530.[31] And was the subject of this work *really* its hero's onanism?[32] Jean Delay, in his capacity as a professional psychiatrist, denies that Gide is as exceptional as he claims in his inability to blend spiritual and sensual relationships.[33] Moreover, this inability was not total, as Gide proved later in his relations with Marc Allégret which are recorded in his *Journal* for 1917 and 1918.

Gide is unfair in his depiction of Heredia. By being constantly compared to Mallarmé, whom Gide idolized, Heredia cannot but suffer.[34] One is also hesitant to believe that Gide would have been really willing to desert his literary friends for the friendship of a natural scientist.[35] And the year after the publication of *Les Cahiers d'André Walter* was not so dissipated as he paints it. He not only wrote *Le Traité du Narcisse* and *Les Poésies d'André Walter*; he also kept a diary and a notebook-record of his prodigious reading, while corresponding frequently with several friends. In each of the diary, notebook, and correspon-

29. Delay, I: 389.
30. See Alain Goulet "Les Premiers Vers d'André Gide", in *Les Cahiers André Gide*, 1 (Paris, 1969), p. 128.
31. See Delay, I: 479.
32. Boisdeffre, *Vie d'André Gide*, I: 140.
33. Delay, I: 534.
34. See Delay, II: 55.
35. *Ibid.*, p. 76.

dence, he speaks of the works he is planning at the time.[36] Georges-Paul Collet has shown an inconsistency in Jacques-Emile Blanche's and Gide's stories of where they met.[37] In the last paragraph of Part One, Gide says that it was at a dinner of the Princesse Ouroussof. Blanche claims that Robert de Bonnières introduced them at his (Bonnières's) home.

Inconsistencies and misconceptions do not decrease in Part Two of the autobiography. Gide is relatively laconic about the two major events of 1891: Madeleine's strongly discouraging refusal of his proposal at the beginning of the year, and his stimulating encounters with Oscar Wilde in December.[38] In the first case, the nature of Part Two is such that there is little place for Madeleine before the closing pages. In the second case, it would appear that Oscar Wilde is to be painted fully only against the background of African cities and landscape. In his heroic account of the liberating gesture of leaving his Bible at home when leaving for Africa, Gide neglects to add that he soon wrote from Montpellier for his mother to send it.[39] He is inexact about the time of the walk in the public garden in Milan which is said to have inspired his *Paludes*. It occurred after his stay in Champel rather than before it.[40] The walk did, however, occur before his stay at La Brévine, which was of two months' duration and not three as he suggests. This Swiss village was to suffer in his treatment of it in both *Si le grain ne meurt* and *La Symphonie pastorale*. The people here were not so unfriendly as Gide describes them. The doctor and the minister seem to have done all that could be reasonably expected of them, and a very willing servant-girl was ready for more than that.[41]

To be convincing, the second African trip required just as honest handling as the first, and yet Pierre de Boisdeffre has considered it untrustworthy in its treatment of Oscar Wilde. For his biography of Gide, Boisdeffre chooses to use material from the earlier *In Memoriam*, claiming that the version in *Si le grain ne meurt* has been touched up, and is hence suspect. As an example, he points out that Gide added blood to the brawl in Blidah in the second version.[42] Lord Alfred Douglas, of course,

36. *Ibid.*, pp. 77-8.
37. Georges-Paul Collet, "André Gide épistolier", in *Entretiens sur André Gide* (La Haye, 1967), p. 70.
38. See Delay, II: 133-4, 274.
39. *Ibid.*, pp. 275-6.
40. *Ibid.*, p. 358.
41. *Ibid.*, p. 381.
42. See Boisdeffre, *Vie d'André Gide*, I: 243n., 245.

protested that everything Gide said about him and Wilde was fabricated, and that if Gide had been English, he would have sued him for libel! [43] In any case, we know that it was only one evening and not several days that Gide spent alone with Wilde in Algiers while Douglas fetched young Ali at Blidah. [44] There is also reason to believe that rather than Marie Leuenberger's threat to leave the Gide family, it was the scandalous publicity surrounding Oscar Wilde's case which kept Gide from taking Athman to Paris. [45] The omission of Gide's prenuptial consultation with the doctor who told him that he would rapidly adjust to heterosexual experiences after his marriage may have been caused by concern for Madeleine's feelings. It turns up finally in *Et nunc manet in te.* [46]

What *are* we to think of all this? Some inconsistencies we have found excusable on the grounds of a faulty memory or because Gide was furnished with incorrect information. Other examples, such as revisions in the letter from Maurice Démarest, are much less so. Just how much licence with the truth can the autobiographer be allowed and still remain worthy of our respect? Jean Delay, who had access to most of the documents pertaining to the years of Gide's life covered in *Si le grain ne meurt,* once again provides an answer. Delay bases his judgement on Gide's remark that it is impossible to recapture in continuous prose the simultaneity of his two-sided personal dialogue. Delay explains that it is this difficulty of composition which has required that Gide the painter simplify the complexity of Gide the model. His lighting of the portrait has illuminated some characteristics at the expense of other contemporaneous ones; and this same lighting has an effect on the people and events that surround the central model. But even so, according to Delay, *Si le grain ne meurt* is a masterpiece of autobiography which on the basis of its exactness of detail alone surpasses analogous efforts. [47] Delay's praise and forgiveness are kind, but they lead us to question the reliability of *any* autobiography if Gide's is comparatively superior in factual authority. His explanation, moreover, is only partially satisfying.

43. R. H. Sherard, *André Gide's Wicked Lies about the Late Mr. Oscar Wilde in Algiers in January, 1895* (Calvi, 1933). See also Peter Hoy's amusing analysis of this preposterous pamphlet, "R. Harborough Sherard, Lord Alfred Douglas, and André Gide's *Si le grain ne meurt*", *Adam*, nos. 337-9 (1970), pp. 52-61.
44. See Delay, II: 455.
45. *Ibid.*, pp. 477-8.
46. *Et nunc manet in te*, p. 1130.
47. Delay, II: 10.

Surely our examples, many of which were originally alluded to by Delay, have shown that Gide's discrepancies have not all been ones of simplification. Their more common characteristic seems to be carelessness, as if Gide felt that the question of accuracy in detail was immaterial to the total impression of a factual self-portrait. Still, simplification and carelessness are less worrisome than deliberate falsification.

Roger Martin du Gard, who was well placed to know, comments that Gide's self-portrait was always slanted with the opinion of posterity in mind.[48] Gide traces not only the self that actually existed, but also aspects of himself which he only believed to exist. Very few people are infallible in their self-appraisal, and even fewer could be counted on for as much honesty as Gide in an autobiography. Gide's factual discrepancies, in Martin du Gard's eyes, would become only normal human failings, associated with the larger question of most people's incapacity for completely honest self-portrayal. They would have little bearing on the total impression of the autobiography. Gide confessed that facts external to himself could indeed become twisted in his memory; but the personal emotion evoked by the events remains constant. His nephew, Dominique Drouin, laughingly pointed out that Gide's 1931 account of a story which Drouin had told him at the end of the First World War so distorted the original version as to become pure invention. In consternation Gide investigated what might have happened, and, somewhat relieved, surmised that while he might have telescoped two different stories, he had not, after all, invented a new one: "Car, en tout cas, ce que je n'avais pu inventer, c'était mon émotion . . ."[49] We may and must believe that even where there are doubtful facts in *Si le grain ne meurt,* the emotions are honest. It would seem that this is all we can hope for from any autobiography. This is especially true when the autobiographer is, as we have seen in the case of Gide, using his own life and a narrative form primarily in the interest of polemics. Provided that the emotional state he associates with each event is honestly depicted, Gide will have fulfilled his obligation to the autobiographical genre.

48. Roger Martin du Gard, *Notes sur André Gide*, in *Oeuvres complètes*, vol. II, p. 1413.
49. *Ainsi soit-il,* p. 1206.

5

The
Novel
in an
Autobiography

IT would seem that it is not only the structure of Gide's autobiography which can
be described in terms of the novel. The liberties he takes with
factual accuracy can also call to mind the word "fiction". In
spite of Gide's essentially honest intentions, the hero of his work
can be nothing but one version of himself. Similarly, the other
figures—his father, his mother,his cousins, aunts, and uncles,
his playmates, schoolmates, and literary friends—are versions
of these people as he saw them, or as he remembers them, or as
he wishes them to have been for the purpose of his work and its
public. We are sometimes dealing not so much with real people
as with literary creations who seem real only because their
author wishes them so. The less these figures resemble their
real-life models, the closer they approach being literary creations, and the closer their author's craft comes to being that of a
novelist. Gide's version of his Uncle Charles is exaggerated
enough that if it were not for his name and certain unalterable
details like a Montpellier address and a professional chair in
political economy, the man painted in *Si le grain ne meurt*
might be considered a fictional invention. In the autobiography, Gide's uncle's unmitigated seriousness is meant as a foil
for his father's gentleness and good humour, and a leavening in
the gruffness could spoil the illusion. Autobiographers are, like
novelists, illusionists, and one of the illusions they create is that
their readers are in fact reading a novel.

Pierre Lafille has pointed out that in reading *L'Immoraliste*
and *Si le grain ne meurt* side by side, a reader can have the

unsettling experience of not being able to distinguish which is the autobiography and which the work of fiction. He finds more fervour and more colour in the earlier *Immoraliste,* and strangely enough, more truth too: "Il [Gide] fait plus vrai en se glissant dans un personnage étranger qu'en se peignant lui-même, volontairement et ouvertement."[1] Lafille also quotes a long, unidentified passage in which in a young lady's room a young man discovers the love of his life.[2] He invites the reader to guess what part of Gide's *ébauches* this could come from, since in style and content it could be a version of the "Alissa" scene in either *La Porte étroite* or *Si le grain ne meurt.* It is, in fact, from Fromentin's *Dominique,* and serves to illustrate the interchangeability of the outward appearance of the two genres, as well as the similarity of the literary values of the two authors concerned.

Nowadays, it is difficult to imagine a subject which is not potentially "novel material". This has not always been the case. As lawless a genre as the novel has always been, there have been certain themes — different ones for different periods — which one associated with fiction more readily than others. This was particularly true at the time of publication of *Si le grain ne meurt.* Some readers of French novels were still devoted to the conservative, bourgeois values of Barrès and Bourget. Others were reading their way through the volumes of Proust, Martin du Gard, Duhamel, and Mauriac which were appearing with considerable regularity throughout the decade of the 1920s. In England, the word novel called forth the names Galsworthy and Arnold Bennett, spoken with awe. And in Canada, Mazo de la Roche was embarking on her *Jalna* series which would for more than one generation stand as the peerless national "novel". All these authors—even Proust—were serving up what the reading public of the twenties wanted: family rivalry, country estates, and promising marriages; revolt from families, struggles for inheritance, and adulterous liaisons. Family life and marriage were useful foundations on which a writer could build his story, as the author of the successful *Symphonie pastorale* well knew. And Norman estates had already contributed to the popularity of *La Porte étroite* and *Isabelle.*

In *Si le grain ne meurt,* just as in these *récits,* Gide used some elements of the fashionable novel as a pretext for his moralizing. The family he presents is larger than any other that he previously painted. Without being statistically complete, his

1. Pierre Lafille, *André Gide romancier* (Paris, 1954), p. 5.
2. *Ibid.,* pp. 405-6.

genealogical details are clear enough that interested readers can reconstruct a rudimentary family tree.[3] La Roque and Cuverville are estates which most of Gide's bourgeois readers would have liked to own, and readers of love stories can find satisfaction in the youthful hero's touching self-dedication to his cousin. Furthermore, their engagement provides the happy ending. Admirers of the revolt of Jacques Thibault from his family hearth can find something similar in the African adventure of the protagonist of *Si le grain ne meurt*; and in general, a sense of the *inquiétude* of adolescence, which had been painted by Alain-Fournier, Radiguet, Cocteau, and Gide himself, is echoed here. In many ways, the work is very much like a *Bildungsroman,* tracing an evolution and awakening from childhood to early manhood. After the narrator-hero's emergence from his vegetative childhood, the story-line follows, in broadest terms, his quest for emotional and intellectual fulfilment.

Certain passages of *Si le grain ne meurt* are particularly reminiscent of similar scenes from famous novels. Little Gide's uncomfortable arrival at the Ecole Alsacienne to the accompanying whispers of "Oh! un nouveau! un nouveau!" (p. 389) reminds us of poor Charles Bovary's unpleasant first day as a new student. Bovary's and Gide's far-from-distinguished classroom performances are also strikingly alike, and the somewhat underhanded dismissal of the young Gide from the Ecole Alsacienne (pp. 390-2) recalls the treatment of Jacques Thibault in *Le Cahier gris.* Gide's schoolboy fights remind one of similar spirited battles in *Le Grand Meaulnes* or Cocteau's *Les Enfants terribles.* The children's fascination with Uncle Henri's factory (pp. 414-15) again recalls Alain-Fournier, this time the blacksmith's shop in Chapter Three of *Le Grand Meaulnes.* Both locations had a mysterious capacity to encourage young imaginations. And little André Gide's adventure with the pious Protestant family near Uzès seems to have taken on an importance not dissimilar to Meaulnes's at the Galais *fête.*

To point out these parallels in novels familiar to Gide is not to say that these passages had strongly or even directly influenced our author's creative processes. Indeed, *Le Cahier gris* (1922) and *Les Enfants terribles* (1929) post-date the composition of the relevant passages in *Si le grain ne meurt.* Moreover, a close comparison of all the related passages would inevitably reveal glaring differences in their purpose, detail, and style. What one

---

3. See Appendix A for a genealogy chart of the Gide and Rondeaux families for the period covered in *Si le grain ne meurt.*

sees here is merely that in selecting material from his life for transmittal to his autobiography, Gide often chose the "stuff" of successful fiction. This is not at all surprising, when one considers that one of André Gide's fundamental *nourritures* was literature, that continually self-spawning art. He could indeed have been inspired to choose some episodes over other possibilities because of some vague but agreeable literary recollections stored in the recesses of his memory; and it is particularly understandable that those lazy early chapters of his autobiography admittedly spun out to fill up a suitable number of pages, might contain vestiges of past reading. The same could be true of his choice of images. Would, for instance, Gide have been likely to describe the descent of his mystical canary as "à la manière du Saint-Esprit" (p. 478), had he not already encountered the ascent of Félicité's parrot in Flaubert's "Un Coeur simple"? There are, however, two novelists whose works were clearly uppermost in his mind at the time of writing *Si le grain ne meurt*. In the case of Stendhal and Marcel Proust, we might even venture to speak of "influence".

It is to these two novelists that Gide refers in his *Journal* on days when he is writing *Si le grain ne meurt*. When his own prose seems to him distastefully tepid, he turns to the letters of Stendhal, whose "pétulance" he finds refreshing.[4] Much later, while writing the tenth chapter of Part One, he was also writing his preface to *Armance*.[5] But had Gide not mentioned Stendhal himself, it would still have been to *Le Rouge et le noir* and *La Chartreuse de Parme* that we would have turned. They are, after all, the most likely French novels to have guided him in composing his novel-like autobiography. We must remember that in 1913, when asked to name the ten best French novels, Gide chose *La Chartreuse de Parme* for the number one position.[6]

4. *Journal*, le 17 décembre 1916, p. 584. Furthermore, Mme van Rysselberghe verifies that Gide read the *Vie de Henry Brulard* on November 11, 1920, specifically in order to take lessons from Stendhal's style. At that time, Gide said: "J'en ai toujours un [un Stendhal], [. . .], c'est mon os de seiche; je m'y fais le bec." *Cahiers de la Petite Dame*, p. 56.

5. *Journal*, le 1er janvier 1921, p. 688. La Petite Dame describes Gide's anger when attacked by Jean Schlumberger over the excessive frankness of the preface. Schlumberger and Jacques Rivière appear to have been apprehensive of the extent to which Gide was preparing to unveil his sexual views and practices, and consequently associated the preface to *Armance* with such projects as *Corydon* and *Si le grain ne meurt*. See *Cahiers de la Petite Dame*, p. 82.

6. "Les Dix Romans français que . . .", in *Incidences* (Paris, 1951), pp. 144-5. Determined that one of Stendhal's novels deserved the number one position, Gide seriously considered *Le Rouge et le noir* before finally deciding on *La Chartreuse*.

What he admired in Stendhal he was going to use—most likely unknowingly—in *Si le grain ne meurt,* his first long narrative work which was too ambitious, too bulky, too descriptive to adopt entirely the form of his own *récits.* This would be the first time that Gide would abandon frame-narrators, diary forms, and sustained oral monologues, and simply divide his work into chapters of almost equal length reminiscent of Stendhal's, albeit longer. Like Stendhal's, each chapter concludes strongly with the promise of future developments.

Le Rouge et le noir may be a "Chronique de 1830", but *La Chartreuse de Parme* is a chronicle of the complete life of Fabrice del Dongo from his conception until he dies, Christ-like, in his thirty-third year. *Si le grain ne meurt* too is a chronicle, told from the birth of its hero to his engagement at the age of twenty-five. In *La Chartreuse* the ironical narrator looks with affection at his sometimes bumbling hero and becomes more than simply a vehicle for recounting the plot; similarly, the narrator of *Si le grain ne meurt,* who looks alternately with exasperation and sympathy at the youthful subject of his story, sustains the work's tone and becomes fully characterized himself. Furthermore, the proportionate quantity of descriptive prose in each of the two works is not dissimilar. Externally at least, *La Chartreuse de Parme* and *Si le grain ne meurt* are sufficiently similar to attract our attention.

Gide's fascination with Fabrice del Dongo was phenomenal. He had even created a brief parody of an episode from *La Chartreuse* for his Prométhée, who was incarcerated as a "fabricant d'allumettes sans brevet" in a prison which from the outside "présentait l'aspect d'une tour".[7] Prométhée's escape thanks to his eagle is a tribute to Fabrice's comical escape from the Tour Farnèse, assisted by the wiles of his Aunt Gina. Gide's most Stendhalian hero is, of course, Lafcadio Wluiki, whose illegitimate birth, personal charm, impulsiveness, and propensity for adventure all remind us of Fabrice.[8] But the first twenty-five years of Gide's own life furnished very little material which paralleled Fabrice's, and in the specific content of *Si le grain ne meurt,* aside from the adventuresome aspect of Part Two, it is

7. *Le Prométhée mal enchaîné,* p. 316.
8. For full studies of Gide's *rapprochements* with Stendhal, see the works listed in the bibliography by Everett Knight, Pierre Lafille, Mohammed-Taghi Ghiassi, and D. A. Steel. To the best of my knowledge none of these works refer to the Stendhalian transposition in *Le Prométhée mal enchaîné.* Nor does Kurt Weinberg's study, *On Gide's "Prométhée": Private Myth and Public Mystification.*

difficult to find textual analogies with *La Chartreuse de Parme*.

It is not too preposterous to suggest, however, that Gide was aware of not only the lack of the petulant Stendhalian style in his work, but also the absence of a Stendhalian hero. In several entries in his diary for the summer of 1917, Gide assumes the name of Fabrice and speaks of himself in the third person. The *Journal* takes on the semblance of prose fiction.[9] "Fabrice" has spent time with the young "Michel" (in real life, Marc Allégret) and seems to be aglow with the triumph of an emotionally and physically successful love affair. Rejuvenated by this new experience, Gide is able to identify himself at last with a Stendhalian hero, and by describing himself as the romantic Fabrice, he may be compensating for the comparative dullness of his autobiography, on which he was currently working. Moreover, it is only after this period that in Part Two Gide attributes to his protagonist some of Fabrice's self-centred energy.

There is a further Stendhalian aspect which must be considered. Much has been made of Gide's distinction between the creative techniques of Dostoevsky and Tolstoy, and his preference for the former.[10] *Les Faux-monnayeurs* is often considered his Dostoevskian novel. It must not be overlooked, though, that Gide based his distinction between the two Russian authors partially on the lighting which they focus on their narrative, and that Gide included Stendhal and Roger Martin du Gard with Tolstoy as novelists who bathe a scene in a single, even projection of light. This is precisely what Gide himself does in his unilinear presentation of the characters and places in *Si le grain ne meurt*. One figure after another moves forward on a fully lit stage to be studied simply, before retiring to make room for his successor. All sides are equally visible for exploration, and the reader comes to know M. Schifmacker and M. de la Nux, Lionel de R. and Armand Bavretel in the same way and to the same degree through their appearances in brightly lit scenes. Gide's lighting, like Stendhal's, is here far removed from Rembrandt's or Dostoevsky's. With this in mind, as well as Gide's well-known tendency to move from one subject to its opposite, from one tone to another in successive works, it is possible to see a new *rapport* between *Si le grain ne meurt* and *Les Faux-monnayeurs*. Was he not, after all, as he was beginning *Les Faux-monnayeurs* in 1919, still writing his own Tolstoian—or Stendhalian—work, *Si le grain ne meurt*? And was he not, therefore, all the more ready to recognize *Les Faux-monnayeurs* as

9. *Journal*, août 1917, pp. 628-30.
10. See Gide's *Dostoïevski*, p. 142, and the *Journal des Faux-monnayeurs*, p. 32.

its Dostoevskian counterpart? Pierre Lafille has pointed to Stendhal's autobiography as a source for the inventory technique in Gide's moral history of Vincent Molinier in *Les Faux-monnayeurs*.[11] It at least seems safe to say that if Gide's novel echoes Stendhal's autobiography, his own autobiography is not without debts to at least one of Stendhal's novels.

While writing *Si le grain ne meurt* at Cuverville, Gide began to make comparisons with the "merveilleux livre de Proust" which he had been rereading to Jean-Paul Allégret in Paris.[12] Marcel Proust's marvellous book had to be *Du côté de chez Swann*, as at the time — January 1918 — Proust's later volumes were not yet published. Without being specific as to why, Gide found that his own work suffered by the juxtaposition. Instinctively, some of the earliest reviewers of *Si le grain ne meurt* also linked Gide's work with *A la recherche du temps perdu*. Fernand Vandérem, for instance, felt that the different people and places in *Si le grain ne meurt* were neither very special nor very picturesque, and were far less interesting than Proust's analogous pages.[13]

It is now fairly normal practice to discuss Gide and Proust together. Their roughly similar birth-dates, their interest in homosexuality, their highly autobiographical subject matter, their innovations in the technique of fiction-writing, and their concern for the role of the writer in his work have all encouraged this. In the 1920s their names were beginning to be linked, although their lives had rarely touched. Gide had, of course, been responsible for the rejection of the original publication of *Du côté de chez Swann* at the N.R.F., and rumour had it that he had perhaps not even opened the manuscript.[14] But shortly after, Gide's admiration for Proust's work became unbounded, and in 1921 their common interest, which would become public knowledge with the publication of *Corydon* and *Sodome et Gomorrhe*, drew them together for two interviews.[15] Moreover, in the naming of two of his characters in *Les Faux-monnayeurs*,

11. Lafille, *André Gide romancier*, p. 426.
12. *Journal*, le 14 janvier 1918, p. 644. Madame van Rysselberghe adds that Gide felt demoralized in the spring of 1921 when he juxtaposed Part Two of *Si le grain ne meurt* with *Le Côté de Guermantes*. She quotes Gide: "Je me fais l'effet d'être d'un sommaire à côté!" See *Cahiers de la Petite Dame*, p. 71.
13. Vandérem, "Les Lettres et la vie", p. 736.
14. See J. Henry Bornecque, "André Gide et *Du côté de chez Swann*", *Bulletin de la Société des Amis de Marcel Proust et des Amis de Combray*, no. 7 (1957), pp. 307-9.
15. These interviews are reported in the *Journal*, mai 1921, pp. 691-4.

Gide perhaps unwittingly paid tribute to his by-this-time-deceased compatriot. La Pérouse, Boris's difficult grandfather, bears the name of both the Paris street on which Odette de Crécy lived, and that of the Paris restaurant in which Charles Swann dined because of its name's association with his elusive mistress; the slippery Robert de Passavant's surname is the motto of the Guermantes family, and is most closely associated with that other gentleman of less than certain virtue, the Baron de Charlus.[16] But in 1926, at the time of publication of *Si le grain ne meurt,* it was still not because of biographical similarities or previous Proustian echoes in Gide's works that one might be drawn to compare Gide's autobiography with *Du côté de chez Swann.* Comparisons arose quite simply out of intrinsic parallels in the texts.

Although there are affinities throughout the whole of both volumes, it is essentially Part One of *Si le grain ne meurt* and the "Combray" section of Proust which invite comparison. Both works are portraits of the artist as a young boy and adolescent. And in both cases, the young boy is hypersensitive, if not neurotic. Young Marcel's trauma about going to bed without his mother's good-night kiss has its answer in young Gide's three *Schaudern.* Both boys live in a mother-oriented world, although there is in neither case any shortage of aunts and uncles. The majority of both families represent rigid moral values, but in Marcel's Uncle Adolphe and Emmanuèle's mother, each family has a notable exception with which to cope. Vacation time is the highlight of both boys' youthful years, and if Marcel's Combray is recalled with more poetry than La Roque, Cuverville, and Uzès, it is not recalled with more love.

From the earliest pages, more specific parallels between the two stories of childhood accumulate. The magic lantern which flashed the story of Geneviève de Brabant and Golo on Marcel's bedroom wall is the single playtoy that stands out in his voluntary recollections of Combray; similarly, a kaleidoscope, "un merveilleux instrument", which also relies on illumination for magic effect, will dominate Gide's childhood memories. Gide even echoes some of Proust's preoccupations with the role of sleep. It is on the threshold of sleep that the young Gide senses a mysterious second world which he can never reach by forcing his way in: "Je ne cherchais pas à percer le mystère; je sentais que j'eusse empêché tout net ce que j'eusse essayé de surprendre" (p. 363). Gide calls this mysterious level of exis-

16. See *A l'ombre des jeunes filles en fleurs* (Livre de poche), p. 344.

tence "une seconde réalité", and it is not to be confused with the
world of dreams: "Et quand je me retrouve dans mon lit, j'ai les
idées toutes brouillées et je pense, avant de sombrer dans le
sommeil, confusément: il y a la réalité et il y a les rêves; et puis il
y a *une seconde réalité*" (p. 362). Gide recalls first sensing this
second reality on an evening of a family ball in Rouen when he
feared being punished for watching from a stairway. His determination to disobey even in the face of probable discipline
recalls Marcel's desperate attempt to summon his mother while
she, like Gide's family, was receiving company. The scene that
the young Gide witnesses is to him incomprehensible and
unreal. Proust's mystical world, which he calls "la vraie vie", is,
of course, not the same as Gide's, but its great inaccessibility is:
"Alors, bien en dehors de toutes ces préoccupations littéraires et
ne s'y rattachant en rien, tout d'un coup, un reflet de soleil sur
une pierre, l'odeur d'un chemin me faisaient arrêter par un
plaisir particulier qu'ils me donnaient, et aussi parce qu'ils
avaient l'air de cacher, au-delà de ce que je voyais, quelque
chose qu'ils invitaient à venir prendre et que malgré mes efforts
je n'arrivais pas à découvrir."[17]

Even Proust's *madeleine* episode has its Gidean counterpart,
although much less is made of it. The nostalgic power of the
taste of the little cake dipped in tea is found in the words and
music of a song used by Gide's mother to straighten out a
recollection of a military parade which her son's voluntary
memory was recalling incorrectly. "Et soudain je reconnaissais
aussi la chanson. Tout se remettait à sa place et reprenait sa
proportion," says Gide (p. 361). Proust had said: "Et tout d'un
coup le souvenir m'est apparu. Ce goût, c'était celui du petit
morceau de madeleine . . ."[18] In both works, too, the protagonist's vocation is given a mystical orientation. It is, for
instance, something mystical in the sight of the "clochers de
Martinville" which inspires Marcel to borrow pencil and paper
from Doctor Percepied to write a description of them. Gide's
mystical signal took the form of a canary which descended like
the Holy Ghost to perch on his cap on New Year's Day, 1884:
"Déjà j'étais enclin à me croire une vocation; je veux dire une
vocation d'ordre mystique; il me sembla qu'une sorte de pacte
secret me liait désormais" (p. 478). And to verify the matter,
several days later he by chance came upon another canary.

The young Marcel and André share more than mystical

---

17. *Du côté de chez Swann* (Livre de poche), p. 214.
18. *Ibid.*, p. 57.

experiences. In both works, considering their dates of composition, there is a singular amount of attention paid to masturbation and lesbianism. Marcel twice recalls his private activities in "le petit cabinet sentant l'iris",[19] for which we have a reply on Gide's opening page and in his suspension from the Ecole Alsacienne. The young Marcel witnesses the surprising behaviour of Mlle Vinteuil and her friend, while young Gide will listen to Marie and Delphine (pp. 385-6). They both recall their early reading of George Sand and their walks with their families, Gide's with his father to the Jardin du Luxembourg or the Jardin des Plantes, or around Uzès, and Marcel's to the Côté de Méséglise or the Côté des Guermantes, or the Bois de Boulogne. Gide's paternal grandmother constantly knitting her unfinished socks is almost as colourful as Marcel's happily hypochondriac Tante Léonie. Marcel's single-minded interest in Gilberte Swann is paralleled by André's love for Emmanuèle, and Marcel's socially ill-adjusted friend Bloch suggests the boorish behaviour of Gide's friend Armand Bavretel (Emile Ambresin) at the Bavretel family receptions. Both authors, who followed with intense interest developments in the Dreyfus Affair, give special attention to their early encounters with the Jewish question. Marcel's grandfather is presented as being playfully anti-Semitic, a characteristic which his grandson, who has a predilection for Jewish friends like Bloch, by no means shares. André Gide seems to have been pleased by how little his cousin Albert's friend Edouard Simon appeared to him to be Jewish (p. 512).

Both families have their faithful and indestructible servants. Marcel's Françoise is described as "immobile et debout dans l'encadrement de la petite porte du corridor comme une statue de sainte dans sa niche."[20] However, it is not for the Gides' maid Marie, but rather for the curious Oulad Naïl prostitutes, that Gide uses Proust's simile: "immobiles, somptueusement vêtues et parées, avec leurs colliers de pièces d'or, leur haute coiffure, elles semblent des idoles dans leur niche" (p. 565). The use of artistic grounds for a simile is in the case of both authors usually a compliment to the person who is the tenor of the analogy. Moreover, the association of an individual with a work of art enhances their interest for Gide almost as much as for Proust. While in Marcel's mind Gilberte Swann is associated with the books of Bergotte, and Odette's charm for Swann depends highly on her resemblance to a figure in a Botticelli

19. *Ibid.*, pp. 16, 189.
20. *Ibid.*, p. 64.

painting and her ability to play (even if poorly) the Vinteuil theme on the piano, Gide associates his Emmanuèle too with literature: "Dans les livres que je lisais, j'inscrivais son initiale en marge de chaque phrase qui me paraissait mériter notre admiration, notre étonnement, notre amour" (p. 496). On looking at his dying mother's hands, Gide's admiration for her increases as he associates her with the arts: "Et soudain, regardant ces pauvres mains que je venais de voir peiner si désespérément, je les imaginai sur le piano, et l'idée qu'elles avaient naguère appliqué leur maladroit effort à exprimer, elles aussi, un peu de poésie, de musique, de beauté . . . cette idée m'emplit aussitôt d'une vénération immense, et tombant à genoux au pied du lit, j'enfonçai mon front dans les draps pour y étouffer mes sanglots" (p. 610).

This survey should be sufficient to show the undeniable affinities between the two works. But is it possible to compare an autobiographical novel with an autobiography without even mentioning their difference in genres? Jean Delay seems to think so, and in fact does so: "Sous un certain angle *Du côté de chez Swann* est l'histoire d'un amour entre un enfant et une mère aimante, *Si le grain ne meurt* l'histoire d'un conflit entre un jeune prévenu et son juge sévère."[21] Both works are in Delay's eyes *stories,* and their interest is the psychological *rapport* of the child with his mother. Both are equally valid on his literary and psychological levels, the latter qualification being in particular no mean achievement. Most readers, however, have preferred *Du côté de chez Swann* to *Si le grain ne meurt.* This is, of course, to a large extent a matter of personal taste. It may also be a matter of genre; for, as Roy Pascal points out, by allowing himself the flexibility of a novelist, Proust has avoided the problem of the autobiographer who can neither "get inside other people nor outside himself."[22] Proust's *A la recherche* may be less honest than *Si le grain ne meurt,* says Pascal, but it is infinitely more profound. In defence of Gide, however, we must add that the lack of an outright polemical purpose in *A la recherche* allowed its author to concentrate fully on the aesthetic and psychological aspects of his work. Proust would have found a defence of homosexuality unthinkable, and in fact did his best to make his homosexual characters unpleasant, or comic, or deeply pathetic. Gide was, nevertheless, quite clearly inspired by the *literary* aspects of *A la recherche,* and incorporated some of them into his autobiography. Even though their genres and purposes are

21. Delay, *La Jeunesse d'André Gide,* II: 535.
22. Pascal, *Design and Truth,* p. 177.

different, outwardly at least the works are similar. We *can,*
then, quite reasonably compare Proust's novel with Gide's
autobiography — but only if we keep in mind the advantages
which Proust's chosen genre and more purely aesthetic position
permitted him.

Gide was aware that one work in particular influenced portions of *Si le grain ne meurt.* This was Edmund Gosse's *Father and
Son,* an autobiography which, like so many others, has been said
to read like fiction. Gide had probably read *Father and Son* as
early as 1910.[23] In Gosse's work, the deeply Calvinistic father
reminds us of Gide's mother and grandfather Tancrède. The
son's interest in biology recalls Gide's own. The Gosse father
and son studying flora and fauna along the English coast are
reminiscent of both Gide's walks with his father and his botanizing with Anna Shackleton. There is evidence in the manuscript
of *Si le grain ne meurt* that Gosse's description of the aquatic
curiosities of Devonshire was uppermost in Gide's mind as he
wrote of his own experiences at Cannes. At this point in the
manuscript there are two *brouillons* of references to *Father and
Son* which never found their way into the published text. The
second one, the longer of the two, is of interest inasmuch as it
throws light on both Gide and Gosse as conservationists:

> Edmund Gosse dans son *Father and Son* parle du merveilleux
> spectacle qu'offraient au temps de sa jeunesse les plages de
> l'Angleterre où son père le naturaliste avait accoutumé de
> chasser et d'herboriser. Plus rien ne reste de tout cela,
> ajoute-t-il, les égouts des villes, les usines, les trafics ont si
> bien emprisonné les eaux.
>
> Hélas! le coeur se serre en songeant avec quelle ingéniosité,
> quelle patience, quelle science, l'homme travaille à enlaidir la
> terre, souvent si belle encore malgré lui! (Bibliothèque Jacques
> Doucet MS *Y* 886-D14)

For both authors, literature becomes an escape from puritanism,
a fact which is apparent in both autobiographies. Gosse had
recognized their biographical affinities while reading *La Porte
étroite*; and while writing *Si le grain ne meurt,* Gide confessed his
indebtedness to Gosse in a letter of October 26, 1917: "Ce que
j'écris à présent (je vous l'ai dit je crois dans ma dernière lettre)
c'est un peu mon *Father and Son.* J'ai compris que je ne parvien-
drais à expliquer ma position vis à vis de certains problèmes

23. For this and further documentation on the Gide-Gosse relationship see
the introduction to *The Correspondence of André Gide and Edmund Gosse.*

religieux et moraux jamais mieux qu'en racontant l'histoire. Non point l'histoire de ces problèmes; mais l'histoire de ma position—si j'ose dire."[24] Gide's indignation was quite understandable when he was asked in a letter from Gosse (who was reading *Si le grain ne meurt*) if he had read *Father and Son*. Of course he had! And Gosse would do well to read on to the parallel passage on flora and fauna![25]

Si le grain ne meurt resembles no author's fiction more than Gide's own. Since Gide had consistently used his own life as the subject of his literature, it is only natural that some of the characters, episodes, allusions, and dictums of his autobiography should seem familiar. The links between *Si le grain ne meurt* and *L'Immoraliste* or *La Porte étroite* are too easily recognizable and too often cited to deserve much mention here. The identification of Michel and Marceline, Jérôme and Alissa with André and Emmanuèle, of La Morinière and Fongueusemare with La Roque and Cuverville, of Michel's honeymoon trip with Gide's emancipatory voyage in 1893, is a simple exercise. Ménalque in one work is Oscar Wilde in another; Bocage is Bocage in both; M. Bucolin's prophecy for Jérôme's hardworking future is Uncle Emile's for Gide; Alissas's lonely death is Anna Shackleton's; and so on. There are, however, echoes of other of Gide's narrative works in *Si le grain ne meurt,* echoes which have been sufficiently neglected to merit our attention.

The parallels begin as early as *Les Cahiers d'André Walter*. In the autobiography, Emmanuèle and André at the bedside of her dying father (p. 580) serve to create the same pathos as the couple with the dying mother in *André Walter*.[26] The busy and colourful port at Toulon (p. 553) is reminiscent of the port at the beginning of *Le Voyage d'Urien*,[27] both inviting the protagonist to exotic places. The illusion that a salt-water pool is a pool of blood (p. 555) reminds one of the mirage of the "Terre Promise" in *El Hadj*,[28] and though less symbolic in the autobiography, it suggests the same evanescent quality that Gide often associates with beauty. Reference to Prométhée (p. 550) proves useful again as Gide compares his youthful puritanism to an eagle which devoured its master as Prométhée's devoured him. The eagle is something he loves, but it eventually becomes a burden. As in *Le Prométhée mal enchaîné*, Gide's eagle is in turn

24. *Gide-Gosse Correspondence*, p. 151.
25. *Ibid.*, p. 187.
26. *Les Cahiers et les poésies d'André Walter* (Paris, 1952), p. 86.
27. *Le Voyage d'Urien*, p. 16.
28. *El Hadj*, p. 358.

destroyed by its master—symbolically—when Gide allows his chastity to give way in Africa. The source of Gide's intimate knowledge of bedbugs which he put to good use in *Les Caves du Vatican* is clearly the camp at Zaghouan (p. 557) where Gide's sleepless night is described with considerably less humour than Amédée Fleurissoire's.[29]

The gestation period of *Les Faux-monnayeurs* somewhat overlaps that of *Si le grain ne meurt*. There is also evidence of an overlap in subject matter. Armand Bavretel, for instance, becomes Armand Vedel in the novel, and Marc de la Nux becomes La Pérouse. The Luxembourg Gardens, site of Gide's walks with his father (pp. 355-6), become a setting for schoolboy gatherings in the novel's first chapter, and elements of life at the Pensions Vedel, Richard, and Keller find their way into the Pension Azaïs-Vedel. The English girls of the Pension Richard become Sarah Vedel's English friend.[30] Rachel Vedel is drawn from Armand Bavretel's self-sacrificing older sister (p. 472). A young boy's persistent masturbation occurs again in the case of Boris, whose adoration of Bronja parallels André's for Emmanuèle. Bernard Profitendieu's encounter with an angel may owe something to Gide's experience with the supposedly heaven-sent canaries (p. 478); and the devil who appears in *Les Faux-monnayeurs* can be none other than the one who is referred to in *Si le grain ne meurt* (p. 549). Finally, when Bernard learns that "il est bon de suivre şa pente pourvu que ce soit en montant,"[31] he is profiting from what Gide the autobiographer tells of learning at the time of his unfortunate article on Henri de Régnier: his initial inclination was better than Vielé-Griffin's advice (p. 539). Gide used the same metaphor of the "pente" to describe his motivation in sleeping with the Oulad Naïls: "Et je voudrais que l'on comprît tout ce qu'il entrait de résolution dans ce qui va suivre; et si l'on tient à ce que *je suivisse ma pente,* que c'était celle de mon esprit et non point celle de ma chair" (p. 564, italics mine).

29. *Les Caves du Vatican,* pp. 775-6.
30. *Les Faux-monnayeurs,* p. 1165. Georges Strauss points out that another source for Miss Aberdeen was surely Marguerite Waddington, the friend of Gide's cousin and sister-in-law, Valentine Rondeaux, "Le Thème des soeurs dans l'oeuvre d'André Gide", in *Les Cahiers André Gide,* 1 (Paris, 1969), p. 250. She might also have been drawn from Gide's contact with the British friends of Elisabeth van Rysselberghe mentioned in the *Cahiers de la Petite Dame, passim.* Sarah herself is a headstrong "modern" girl not unlike Elisabeth.
31. *Les Faux-monnayeurs,* p. 1215.

Among the novelists whom Gide's autobiography has called to mind have been Stendhal, Flaubert, Proust, Alain-Fournier, Martin du Gard, Cocteau, and, of course, Gide himself. His constant literary immersion — particularly in the sea of fiction — is undeniably evident in *Si le grain ne meurt*. In structure and content, Gide's autobiography seems to be almost every inch a novel, while still convincing us that it is an accurate portrait of himself. It may be true that only people who have led eventful lives publish autobiographies, and therefore at the core of every published autobiography is the material for a novel. Few autobiographies, however, can invite comparison with as many formidable novelists as we have discussed here. And the fact that Gide's withstands the analogies so well explains why it has also sustained its reputation among the masterpieces of its genre.

Conclusion

AS OUR point of departure, we chose to emphasize that in spite of Gide's constant references to his "Mémoires", *Si le grain ne meurt* is an autobiography. We have maintained that people and places have taken on an importance in the work only in so far as they reveal truths about Gide himself. Such was the method of writing about his past which best suited his purposes.

There is, however, one very curious chapter in which Gide departs from this procedure. When, in Chapter Ten of Part One, Gide tells of the young literary figures whom he met in the salons of Mallarmé and Heredia, the sudden externalization of their presentation jars with the rest of the narrative. Each one is presented after the fashion of a La Bruyère portrait, and their influence on Gide in any respect other than literary is minimal. This chapter is unique in the work. Even the long development of Oscar Wilde in Part Two includes nothing that does not add to our understanding of the Gidean personality. Chapter Ten would be at home in a volume of *mémoires* in the strictest sense, but its strange unsuitability here only serves to reinforce our notion that the rest of *Si le grain ne meurt* is an autobiography.[1]

---

1. Gide has been mildly reproached as a memorialist in a letter from Albert Mockel in 1924 quoted in the catalogue of the Gide exhibition held in the Bibliothèque Royale Albert Ier in 1970 (item 279). Mockel, who had just read Chapter Ten of Gide's autobiography in the *Nouvelle Revue Française*, found him unnecessarily cruel in his presentation of André Fontainas.

The kind of confusion that can arise in differentiating memoirs from autobiography can also occur when discussing autobiography and autobiographical fiction, where the margin of difference can be every bit as slim. Wayne Shumaker says of *Father and Son,* the autobiography of Sir Edmund Gosse, that it "has the form of a brilliant novel";[2] and the fictional *Du côté de chez Swann* reads like nothing else but an autobiography of childhood. Of course we all *know* that *Father and Son* is an autobiography, and that *Du côté de chez Swann* is a novel. And when Proust biographers and critics begin to convince us that *A la recherche du temps perdu* contains nothing but material from Proust's own life, and that the precious way he writes was the way he *naturally* wrote, and perhaps even thought, all we have to do is remind ourselves that, for instance, Marcel Proust had a brother, while the hero of the novel is an only child. . . . *A la recherche* is not, then, autobiography, but falls into that category of fiction described as "autobiographical". It may be just as factual as some thoroughbred autobiographies; but Proust and others like him have had absolutely no *commitment* to factual accuracy, unlike the autobiographers (some of whom have little enough). Proust has just coincidentally chosen to follow some events of his life in his novel. This was his privilege as a novelist, but not an obligation.

If André Gide's autobiography reads like a novel, it could be argued that this is merely characteristic of the genre. However, *Si le grain ne meurt* reads like a *good* novel, a phenomenon that is not at all common to the genre, and which is attributable to the coincidence that its author is a first-rate novelist. The question arises, then, as to why a successful novelist chose to write an autobiography for his defence of homosexuality rather than use the genre to which he owed his reputation. There would seem to be several reasons.

The most obvious is that the expense of personally damning confessions leaves no doubt as to the importance which the author is giving to his subject. Contrary to advice from Wilde and Proust, and only too aware of the accusations that would be made, Gide *was* ready to use the pronoun "je" to reveal all. Moreover, he would not this time use any interposed narrator named Michel to put the reader off his track.

In the second place, as a propagandist, Gide was to use more than one literary genre. His autobiography would take its place beside the arguments of the *Corydon* dialogues and the example

---

2. Wayne Shumaker, *English Autobiography: Its Emergence, Materials, and Form* (Berkeley, 1954), p. 123.

of Edouard's and Olivier's relationship in *Les Faux-monnayeurs* as yet another rendering of his request for understanding.

In the third place, as Gide uses the genre of autobiography, superficially it differs very little from what his *récits* had already been providing for his readers. The length of his work and its commitment to honesty are the most apparent departures from subject matter and a narrative technique with which he was already comfortable and which pleased his public. And this time, he was eased of the burden of creating a fictitious narrator or explaining how the narrator came to have the inclination, time, or talent to tell his story.

The fresh problems that autobiography imposed were not insurmountable. Gide soon recognized that total accuracy of recollection was neither possible nor necessary. The autobiographer's usual problem of appearing more reliable when treating recent events than childhood was not his, since even the end of his narrative had taken place in the fairly distant past. He had also had time to appraise the retrospective significance of events which may have seemed unimportant at the time, and even the relatively short time-span of his story allowed for sufficient evolution in his own character to keep the readers interested. The problem of characterizing himself both as a young boy and as a mature writer seemed to take care of itself, since personal t its linking his youth and his maturity were different enough to make the connection striking, yet similar enough to keep it believable. The sleepy childhood of the writer with encyclopaedic interests is, for instance, fascinating; yet their constant literary interests, sensitivity, and imagination make both the narrator and his subject unmistakably the same person. And finally, the usual pre-eminent handicap of autobiography becomes for Gide an advantage. For him, the fact that the only character whom the narrator can know thoroughly—if not completely—is himself relieves him of the responsibility of the full development of other characters, and allows him to concentrate on the single example he needs for his purpose, namely himself. Gide's pledge to his mission led to his painting his self-portrait with particularly consistent care, but still an impressive number of secondary figures populate the work.

The end for which *Si le grain ne meurt* was originally written seems to have by now been more or less permanently resolved. Homosexuality is meeting with increasing public tolerance; outmoded legislation is being almost universally modified. In the world of letters, Gide's moral critics, then, have become anachronistic. Furthermore, those probing biographers who used to read *Si le grain ne meurt* solely for information are being satisfied elsewhere; the liberal modern morality to which Gide himself can be credited with contributing has thrown discretion to the winds, so that even Gide's intriguingly libidinous Daniel B. has been identified.[3]

Now that the work can at last be regarded from an unobstructed literary perspective, let us begin by recognizing its genre correctly — literary autobiography. In 1926 it both reinvigorated the genre and set new standards for frankness. Since then, the number of autobiographies by French men of letters has proliferated, and authors like Jean Genet have far outdistanced André Gide in frankness. But over the years, Gide's work has never become just another crumbling landmark in literary history. Nor will it. *Si le grain ne meurt* has the lasting freshness of a classic; and it is time to acknowledge that it is not to its daring subject matter or to its biographical usefulness that it owes its durability, but to the unique personality and literary deftness of the artist who lived its story and recorded it.

3. Maria van Rysselberghe reveals him to be Eugène Rouart, who grew to be the stuffy public figure who may have inspired Gide's portrait of *Robert*. See *Cahiers de la Petite Dame,* p. 360.

APPENDIX A

Genealogy of
André Gide
for the Period Relevant to
Si le grain ne meurt

1. THE PATERNAL LINE

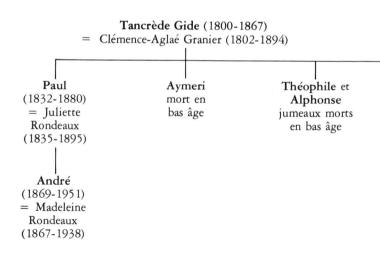

Tancrède Gide (1800-1867)
= Clémence-Aglaé Granier (1802-1894)

Paul
(1832-1880)
= Juliette
Rondeaux
(1835-1895)

Aymeri
mort en
bas âge

Théophile et
Alphonse
jumeaux morts
en bas âge

André
(1869-1951)
= Madeleine
Rondeaux
(1867-1938)

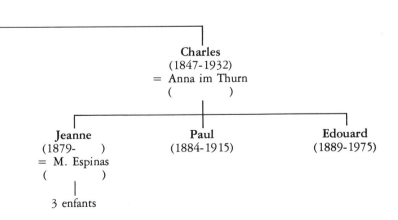

Charles
(1847-1932)
= Anna im Thurn
(   )

Jeanne
(1879-   )
= M. Espinas
(   )

3 enfants

Paul
(1884-1915)

Edouard
(1889-1975)

II. THE MATERNAL LINE

Charles Rondeaux (de Montbray) (1753-1820)

= 1. 1774 Constance Chapaïs (1753-1777)

Jean-Baptiste
(1775-1864)
= Aimée-Césarine Thieullen
(1787-1869)

Constant
(1777-1841)

3 enfants

Charles
(1820-1890)
= Sophie
Fornage
(1826-1880)

Claire
(1822-1901)
= Guillaume
Démarest
(1808-1879)

Jeanne
(1858-1875)

Charlotte
(   )
= Francis
Fenwick

Charles
(1862-1933)

Maurice
(1844-1921)
= Hélène
Alibert

Albert
(1848-1906)
= Marie

3 filles

1 fille

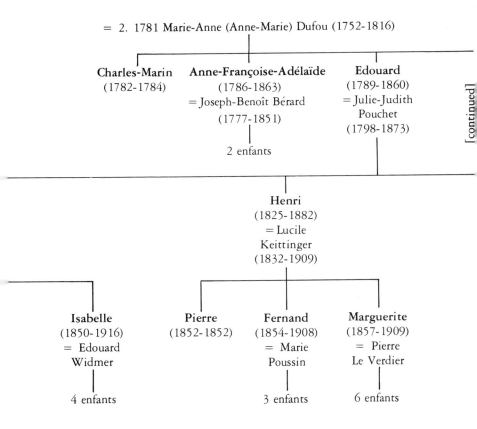

= 2. 1781 Marie-Anne (Anne-Marie) Dufou (1752-1816)

Charles-Marin (1782-1784)

Anne-Françoise-Adélaïde (1786-1863) = Joseph-Benoît Bérard (1777-1851)

2 enfants

Edouard (1789-1860) = Julie-Judith Pouchet (1798-1873)

[continued]

Henri (1825-1882) = Lucile Keittinger (1832-1909)

Isabelle (1850-1916) = Edouard Widmer

4 enfants

Pierre (1852-1852)

Fernand (1854-1908) = Marie Poussin

3 enfants

Marguerite (1857-1909) = Pierre Le Verdier

6 enfants

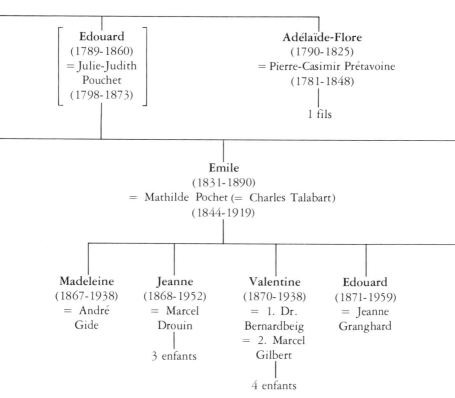

Edouard
(1789-1860)
= Julie-Judith
Pouchet
(1798-1873)

Adélaïde-Flore
(1790-1825)
= Pierre-Casimir Prétavoine
(1781-1848)

1 fils

Emile
(1831-1890)
= Mathilde Pochet (= Charles Talabart)
(1844-1919)

Madeleine
(1867-1938)
= André
Gide

Jeanne
(1868-1952)
= Marcel
Drouin

3 enfants

Valentine
(1870-1938)
= 1. Dr.
Bernardbeig
= 2. Marcel
Gilbert

4 enfants

Edouard
(1871-1959)
= Jeanne
Granghard

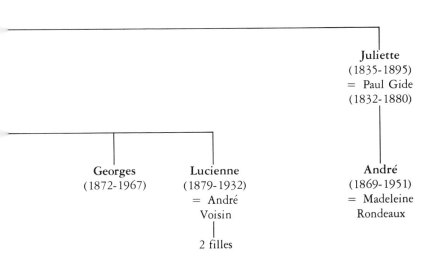

Juliette
(1835-1895)
= Paul Gide
(1832-1880)

Georges
(1872-1967)

Lucienne
(1879-1932)
= André
Voisin

2 filles

André
(1869-1951)
= Madeleine
Rondeaux

Notes to Appendix A

The chief sources of information have been the works by Lavondès, Le Verdier, Nobécourt, and Rufenacht listed in the bibliography. The *lacunae* exist for several reasons. The Gide family history is less well documented than the Rondeaux, since the best source, the Lavondès work, is written for reasons other than genealogical. On the other hand, the Rondeaux family history, published in 1927 by André Gide's first cousin by marriage Pierre Le Verdier, is exceedingly helpful. It is, however, guilty of sacrificing completeness of documentation to the preservation of family prejudices and quarrels. The wife and one daughter of Gide's Uncle Charles Rondeaux, for instance, are not mentioned, as his marriage met with family disapproval. Le Verdier also omits the dates of the other Charles Rondeaux offspring. Similarly, he makes no mention of Albert Démarest's wife and child, whose existence we are aware of thanks to *Si le grain ne meurt*. Madeleine Gide's youngest sister, Lucienne, does not appear, probably because when still an infant she accompanied the "infamous" future Madame Charles Talabart at the time of her separation from Emile Rondeaux. In general, Le Verdier's reasons for writing the history of the Rondeaux family went further than simply the documentation of local history. The work is characterized by smug pride in the family's commercial success, and self-righteousness about their piety and charity. Le Verdier devotes one sentence to his cousin, André Gide, the "amoraliste". There seem to have been good personal grounds, then, for Gide's famous "Familles, je vous hais"; nevertheless, his characteristic ambivalence about his family is reflected in *Si le grain ne meurt*: While his kind treatment of Albert Démarest's private life was generous to the point of daring, considering the circumstances, he omits mention *entirely* of Charles Rondeaux and little Lucienne, thus perhaps inadvertently catering to the traditional family dissension.

Le Verdier tells us that Edouard Rondeaux (the brother of Madame André Gide) was a bachelor. This was doubtless the case in 1927, but Rufenacht mentions a wife.

Félix-Archimède Pouchet falls outside the range of this family tree. He was a first cousin of Gide's maternal grandmother. His son Georges was thus André Gide's second cousin once removed.

The names of several of André Gide's first cousins have been changed in the definitive edition of *Si le grain ne meurt*. Madeleine, Jeanne, and Valentine Rondeaux have become Emmanuèle, Suzanne, and Louise respectively. Fernand Rondeaux becomes Robert; and Isabelle Rondeaux-Widmer's infant son Raoul becomes Emile.

Finally, a tour of the relevant graveyards can be rewarding. In the spring of 1972, for instance, the deplorable state of the Charles Rondeaux family tomb at Asnières contrasted all too significantly with the well-kept Widmer plot at Essonnes.

APPENDIX B

*Notes
on the Manuscript of*
Si le grain ne meurt

SINCE at least the time of Malherbe there has been a widespread notion that to write well one must rewrite, rework, correct, and cross out. Antoine Albalat, for instance, quotes both Chateaubriand and Mme de Staël as recommending a study of the many revisions in the manuscripts of the great authors of the past in order to see a great mind at work.[1] From these recommendations, M. Albalat falls into the trap of deducing that the disorderly manuscripts of Chateaubriand, Flaubert, Bossuet, Pascal, Rousseau, or Buffon are evidence of great writing, while the relatively tidy manuscripts of Stendhal, Massillon, George Sand, Gautier, Mme de Staël, Lamartine, and Dumas *père* suggest lazy or less inspired talent. Jean Prévost bids caution at this somewhat simplistic approach to manuscript study, reminding us that a page without *ratures* may very well have undergone many revisions in the author's mind before being committed to paper.[2] On the other hand, an obviously reworked page informs us of nothing more than that its reader has been allowed to witness the evolution of an idea's expression from very early in its formation. A well-worked-over manuscript may, then, indeed indicate that its author is a conscientious craftsman concerned with *le mot juste*; but a clean manuscript does not indicate the contrary.

The manuscript of *Si le grain ne meurt* is far from tidy. Claude

1. Antoine Albalat, *Le Travail du style enseigné par les corrections manuscrites des grands écrivains* (Paris, 1903), pp. 1-3.
2. Jean Prévost, *La Création chez Stendhal* (Paris, 1951), pp. 38-9.

Martin describes it as "le beau manuscrit . . . couvert de ratures, de repentirs, de variantes, de corrections de toutes sortes."[3] It is certainly all of that; and indeed one would hope, as M. Martin suggests, that some day a critical edition may compare and analyse all the variants from manuscript to final edition. One might hope, too, for a categorization of these variants according to their linguistic nature and their conceptual or stylistic effect, somewhat after the fashion of Irène Vildé-Lot's study of *Les Nourritures terrestres*.[4] This would be no easy task, for in Chapter One alone there are 241 variants between the manuscript and the Pléiade edition, and these changes came about in a variety of intervening editions.[5]

At present, we must limit our interest to purely substantive changes from manuscript to later editions of *Si le grain ne meurt*. While Gide added very little to his manuscript version, he suppressed in printed editions passages of various length. These passages which are extant in the manuscript were in many cases also in the private edition of 1920-1; but the rarity of this edition has rendered them to all intents and purposes inaccessible. The notes in this appendix summarize chapter by chapter the significance of these particular omissions, as well as a few of the more noteworthy factual substitutions. Their discussion sheds further light both on events in the life of André Gide and on his attitude towards his autobiography. For each passage discussed, a page reference is made to its relevant location in the

3. Claude Martin, "Etat présent des études gidiennes 1951-1963", *Critique* xx (juillet 1964): 601.
4. Irène Vildé-Lot, "André Gide et l'art d'écrire d'après les variantes des *Nourritures terrestres* et de quelques autres oeuvres de jeunesse", *Le Français Moderne* xxviii (1960): 259-86; xxix (1961): 29-42, 121-83, 206-22.
5. Surely one of the most useful sources is the copy of the 1924 edition of *Si le grain ne meurt* which Gide used when preparing the text for his *Oeuvres complètes* edition (vol. x, 1936). This copy was item 11 in the catalogue for the sale of the *Archives Arnold Naville concernant André Gide* at the Hôtel Drouot, February 8, 1973. The catalogue informs us that this copy contains numerous indications of passages to be suppressed as well as an important subsequently discarded addition to the paragraph which begins "Pour moi, qui ne comprends le plaisir que . . ." (Pléiade, p. 596). Apparently the addition explicitly clarified *and modified* the meaning of the present single-sentence paragraph.

   The same catalogue describes an essential copy of the 65th edition of *Si le grain ne meurt* (Paris: N.R.F., 1933): "Exemplaire comportant 165 corrections autographes d'André Gide. Ce sont, outre des indications typographiques, des indications pour le rétablissement de certains passages de l'édition de 1924 et des additions — scabreuses — qui n'ont jamais été reproduites" (item 14 in the catalogue).

Pléiade edition. Also, MS is the abbreviation for manuscript and FE stands for the First Edition of 1920-1.

PART ONE

Chapter One

Page 350, after "tous les pâtés." A short paragraph on Gide's lack of success in searching for echoes of his childhood cruelty in his adult behaviour. Crossed out in the manuscript. Presumably Gide did not want to attract attention at this point to his adult self. This suppression is also in accord with his general tendency to minimize the mature narrator's commentary.

Page 350, after "me punir." Another paragraph on the lack of explanation for this sadism which as an adult he finds foreign to himself. Crossed out, doubtless for the same reasons as above.

Page 351, after "c'est-à-dire tout seul." Two sentences describing the elegant stairway of the rue de Tournon. Not in FE. This suppression abbreviates the description.

Page 351. Inserted on a separate sheet of pink paper is a reference to a conversation with Jacques-Emile Blanche, who had said that he had never played marbles as a child: "Pauvre Blanche! C'est vraiment triste d'être si riche, si bien né, si avantagé et de n'avoir jamais joué aux billes!" Not in FE. This is the sort of commentary Gide reserves for his *Journal.*

Page 352, after "trois ou quatre verroteries." A sentence referring to Gide's preference for the simple over the complex, using the example of a quartet or trio as being for him preferable to a full orchestra. Crossed out in MS. This reference to music may explain the choice of the word "accord" in the following sentence.

Page 356, after "débiter des fadeurs." Three sentences explain that the young Gide could not understand what the audience appreciated in the show in the *café-concert,* and that had his father suggested going in and sitting with these people, he would have been instinctively ashamed. Not in FE. Suppression of moral judgement leaves the emphasis on the idyllic aspect of this adventure with his father.

Page 357, after "bien soulagé." A short paragraph recounting his recollection of a young boy at Mme Lackerbauer's who announced that in wartime one ate carriage-horses and drank ink. This passage, which emphasizes the young Gide's extreme gullibility, does not appear in FE.

Page 357, after "à l'autre du morceau." A sentence which explains that the young Gide later compared Mlle de Goecklin to the painter in water-colours of *Nicholas Nickleby.* Crossed out in MS, perhaps because the impression belonged neither to the days described in the passage nor to his point of view as a mature narrator.

Page 357, after "dans la seconde pièce, le piano". Crossed out is an anecdote which describes Mlle de Goecklin's sister passing furtively through the room where the piano lesson was taking place in order to sit in the first room where she worked on artificial flowers or pearl embroidery. Young Gide would nod at her and blush, and she would shrink. Gide perhaps saw that his first chapter was in danger of becoming "Grand Guignol" and thus suppressed the passage.

Page 360, after "me pénétrait le côté . . ." A paragraph developing the description of the house on the rue de Crosne is crossed out in MS, doubtless for the sake of concision.

Page 361, after "majorité de leur fille:" A sentence denying any wish to present himself as a precocious child. Not in FE. The sentence is slightly irrelevant to the passage in which it was placed.

Page 364, after "sa soeur aînée." Two paragraphs and a footnote outlining the snobbery which had existed in the early years of Anna Shackleton's life with the Rondeaux family. In spite of the wishes of Juliette Rondeaux, Mlle Shackleton was given an uncomfortable bedroom, and Claire Rondeaux was unwilling to share the seat of honour in a carriage with her sister's governess. The footnote describes the physical changes made to the house by Henri Rondeaux. This passage and the note are in the FE but are subsequently suppressed, perhaps because there is inaccurate chronology in the suggestion that at the time Claire Rondeaux was not yet married. Moreover, the situation described here was only temporary, Mlle Shackleton being warmly received by the whole family in later years.

Page 365, after "de la société rouennaise". The sentence continues with a reference to Guillaume Démarest's gifts which he sent with a teasing note to his unmarried sister-in-law, Juliette, "à chaque fête de Sainte-Catherine." Also in FE. Suppression difficult to explain except for the fact that since M. Démarest has not yet been identified in the text, his sudden presence here is somewhat unsettling.

Page 366, after "passablement l'italien." MS contains what seems to be an unrelated page. It explains his method of composition and states clearly that his purpose is other than to write a family history. Not in FE. Probably an *ébauche* for the paragraph which begins "J'écrirai mes souvenirs" (p. 360).

Chapter Two

The manuscript for pages 374 to 384 inclusive of the Pléiade edition has not been available for consultation. For these pages, the First Edition has been collated with the Pléiade.

Page 380, after "de couleur inattendue." A sentence in the FE explains that the Sarbonnet has been razed to put a straight road through its site. This commentary probably seemed to Gide distracting in the midst of his recollections, hence its suppression.

Page 388, after "s'endormait-elle?" The sentence, "Un romancier n'aurait jamais permis cela," in the FE (but not in the MS or the Pléiade) attracts the reader's attention to the fact that his narrator is a writer who is conscious that his mother's lapse in vigilance over her son would be considered inconsistent characterization in a novel. Gide suppresses this digression to focus attention on Constance.

Page 388. Another of Constance's songs is crossed out in the manuscript:

> C'était une pauvre fille
> Qui m'a fait pipi
> Qui m'a fait pitié
> Car elle était toute remplie
> De caca caca
> De calamités.

The quotation leaves no doubt as to the extent to which Constance's songs stuck in Gide's memory. The MS continues after "et la pire vulgarité" with an anecdote about a vulgar poster which the young Gide bought along with the expensive sheet-music for a song with the promising title of "Ah! qu'elle sent bon Alexandrine". He defiantly paraded these acquisitions in front of his mother without showing how they had disappointed and disgusted him. He comments that at that time his character seemed decidedly unpromising. This whole section is marked in pencil, "réserver".

Chapter Three

Page 394, after "y nichait." A short paragraph describes the two attractive little corner towers "affectées aux usages que l'on devine." This also appears in FE, but may have been later omitted as being inconsistent with the generally lofty tone of the description of La Roque.

Page 395, after "et tempéré d'un parc." One sentence describing the autumn sunset has been omitted. Still present in FE.

Page 401, after "le goût du travail." Two sentences which further indicate that the cause of his dismissal from the Ecole Alsacienne seemed to have been forgotten, and that his guardian angel was drawing him out of his torpor. Not in FE. Suppressed perhaps because the passage opens up two themes — masturbation and the devil-angel struggle — which he is not ready to pursue here.

Page 403, after "à cette comédie." A redundant sentence (see p. 401) explaining that he had repeated *la neuvième* at the Ecole Alsacienne. Not in FE.

Page 407. The manuscript (*γ* 886-F86-94) contains two other quite different versions of the children's costume ball. It would appear that at one time Gide wanted to present the story of the costumes within a section on his paternal grandmother (where she has difficulty hearing both him and his mother). At another time, it appears that it was to be used as an example of his capacity for infatuation (with the clown) without real desire for physical contact.

Page 407, after "qui s'appelait Roseau." Two sentences referring to his faithful nightly reading of the New Testament in a moleskin-bound edition given to him by his mother. Also in FE with a stylistic variant. Probably later suppressed as not being relevant to the paragraph's central subject — the other *pensionnaires.*

Chapter Four

Page 413, after "maison normande." A good full page of detail describes Gide's cousin Marguerite Rondeaux's artwork, as well as presenting some recollections about her and her brother Fernand. Both cousins were about fifteen years older than Gide, and hence not very close to him. Marguerite was sweet and pious; Fernand was lazy (in his work at the factory), and a spendthrift who could be taken in by the Paris merchants who encouraged his vanity. Gide recalls terrible domestic scenes which occurred when Fernand's parents were obliged to pay their son's debts. The passage ends with an acknowledgement of Fernand's stability as an adult; but after the FE the passage is omitted, probably as a kindness to Gide's Rondeaux relatives.

Page 414, after "d'y aller seuls." A short paragraph which indicates that Fernand was proud of showing off his family's factory to his younger cousins. Gide comments that the factory would no longer seem like very much at the time of his writing.

Not in FE. The presence of the passage compromised the contrast between the forbidden factory and the storehouse, where the children played freely.

Page 415, after "l'avoir connu!" A short passage indicates that Georges Pouchet was rejected as a suitor by Juliette Rondeaux because she had found him impious. Not in FE. In published editions Gide reserves his discussion of Georges Pouchet for later.

Page 417, after "au feu du ciel." A long passage discusses days in M. Tabourel's private tutorials at La Roque when the young Gide watched a butterfly develop disappointingly slowly from chrysalis to adult. On the day of the butterfly's emergence, he became ecstatic, even though he knew what to expect. Failing to understand the boy's sensitivity to the beauty of the phenomenon, M. Tabourel reproached him for his ignorance about natural science, and lost his student's respect. Also in FE. M. Tabourel is omitted entirely in later editions, perhaps because the number of inept or unsuccessful tutors was sufficient without him.

Page 418, after "son cabinet de travail." The MS description of the Charles Gide apartment at Montpellier is fuller than in the FE or subsequent editions. Perhaps trimmed in the interests of brevity.

Page 419, after "le temps de Rabelais." Four or five sentences emphasize the primitive nature of the *lycée* building by telling of a dog or dogs entering freely from the street. Also in FE. The imprecision of Gide's memory as to whether the dog (or dogs) were summoned by the students, came on their own, or belonged to the *concierge*, doubtless encouraged him simply to suppress the whole incident.

Page 421, after "laisseront tranquille." A sentence adds that Mme Gide informed her son that a constitutional representation was formed by the Chamber of Deputies and the Senate, an explanation that helped the boy's understanding not at all. Not in FE. Suppressed as the story stands up better without it.

Page 429. "Je renonce à copier ici les pages où je racontais d'abord Gérardmer." The pages Gide wrote about Gérardmer are extant in an envelope marked "n'a pas servi. — 2e séjour à Lamalou—Gérardmer; les leçons de danse" (γ886-O181-185). Besides the woods at Gérardmer, Gide recalls a lending library in a stationery store where the crippled manager was the author of a book on nature which highly appealed to the young boy. Recollection of a ball at the hotel at Gérardmer sets off a digression on his earlier discomfiture at dancing lessons in

Paris. Gide also recalls a recent trip with his wife to Gérardmer, which proved to be disillusioning except for the amusement provided by legions of tiny frogs on the lakeshore.

Another section in the same place in the manuscript gives further information about the second trip to Lamalou. Here Gide's mother used the example of other patients to teach her son a lesson about "the wages of sin". One of the patients is presented in two versions, one of which involved a conversation between Gide mother and son. The blind patient is sitting in the sun. "S'il ne s'était pas amusé dans sa jeunesse, ça ne serait pas venu du tout, disait-elle en m'emmenant." The reason for suppressing these pages may have been more personal than the fact that, as Gide claims in the published edition, they add nothing new.

Chapter Five

Page 433. The rue de Lecat episode. Gide had many problems with this passage. Particularly difficult was the part where he was going to say that he understood nothing of what was happening in Mathilde Rondeaux's private life. Gide tried to emphasize his own lack of perspicacity, and in a long passage in the MS he explains that if he did not like his aunt, it was in imitation of his mother, rather than out of any critical sense of his own. His mother explained nothing of Mathilde's conduct to her son, and he would not have understood anyway. But he did overhear her reproaching Mathilde for first neglecting her children and then paying excessive attention to the second daughter whom she had accompany her on a trip the previous summer. Also in the MS, Gide confesses to having invented the Lucile Bucolin episode in *La Porte étroite*. He offers as the truth an episode in which his aunt called him close to her while she played on the piano some sensuous music fashionable at the time. Amidst the several manuscript drafts he also confesses that he is unable to recall precisely what he saw in his aunt's room on the crucial day when he returned unexpectedly to her house. Nor can he remember what he and Madeleine said in her room. The version that Gide finally used in the FE (and in the Pléiade) is, we assume, the one he finally wrote so quickly in December 1916.

Page 436, after "une magnificence orientale." Gide was about to speak here of Edmund Gosse's comparable passages on botanizing in *Father and Son*. He continues (after "question de travail?") to speak of the industrial pollution to landscape which Gosse saw in England. After some remarks on his concern for conservation in France, Gide comments that he remains convinced that as a natural scientist he could have made a valuable contribution. Not in FE. Suppressed perhaps as being excessive commentary.

Page 438, after "un instant ma torpeur." A continuation of the sentence states that Gide recognizes in these special moments the first indication of the wings of the angel which will lift him from his shadowy existence. The next paragraph begins with an apology for telling of these incidents outside their chronological order, but other events seem to be "puérilités avoisinantes" by comparison. Also in FE. Perhaps omitted because his linking of the events to religion through the reference to the angel's wings is somewhat misleading.

Page 438, after "Anna déjeunait avec nous." In the first version, the next sentence makes the cause of Gide's *Schaudern* not the death of the Widmer child, but that of a little niece of Anna Shackleton. This is promptly corrected in the MS.

Page 442, after "sa voix me ravissait." A sentence states that Albert Démarest represented for Gide "l'art, la franchise, la liberté." Also in FE. Perhaps suppressed because the tone and content of Gide's discussion of his cousin make the sentence superfluous.

Page 443. The first paragraph of the new section originally began with a brief description of the new apartment in the rue de Commaille. Not in FE. Description withheld until the next chapter and reorganized.

Page 444, after "dans ma mémoire." A sentence develops the idea that the whole Richard (Bauer) household was afraid of Mme Bertrand (Garnier), and it was probably for this reason that the young Gide valued her esteem more highly than that of the others. Also in FE. Suppression difficult to explain, except that Gide may have felt that the sentence suggests that he too was afraid of Mme Bertrand, which was certainly not the case. In the MS the Marché de la Madeleine is mentioned rather than the Marché de Saint-Sulpice which occurs in FE and Pléiade.

Page 449, after "de vous considérer." The story of the padlock and the birds has a lengthier conclusion, in which Gide silently presents Mme Bertrand with the second padlock and key. Only her tea, which is cooling, prevents her from starting up her tirade again. Not in FE. The suppression again makes for a tighter narrative and a more effective conclusion to the story.

Page 450. In the MS the youngest Richard (Bauer) brother's age is given as "2 ou 3 ans de plus que moi." It is "cinq ans de plus" in FE and Pléiade.

Chapter Six

Page 456, after "toutes vos trioles?" A sentence comments that at the time of writing Gide no longer played Mendelssohn, but was even more enthusiastic about what Marie called "trioles". Not in FE. Perhaps suppressed as being excessive commentary.

Page 457. In the MS, M. Merriman (O'Kelly) had his piano student study each piece four measures at a time rather than eight. Eight in FE.

Page 457, after "par une amie." A short discourse by Mme Gide's friend on M. Schifmacker's great accomplishment in making her appreciate music. Also in FE. Suppressed perhaps because in a work which uses relatively little direct discourse, its presence here gives inappropriate importance to this lady.

Page 459, after "malaxer la mélodie." One sentence: "Au demeurant c'était un brave homme." Not in FE. Evidently Gide had decided that Schifmacker was not so "brave" after all, or else decided to leave commentary till the very end of the Schifmacker episode.

Page 460, after "une partie de canotage." The sentence continues with a comment that M. Schifmacker's accident inspired some macabre jokes. Not in FE. Suppressed doubtless in the interests of good taste.

Pages 461-2. Several attempts at the description of the apartment in the rue de Commaille exist in the MS. In one of these Gide tries to remember whether or not every second Sunday when his Aunt Claire and Cousin Albert came to dinner his mother removed the *housses* from the living-room furniture. He decides that she probably left them on. Not in FE.

Page 465. In the MS, Anna Shackleton is included with his mother as considering Chopin's music unhealthy. Not in FE. By limiting the blame for his being forbidden Chopin to his mother, Gide avoids doing disservice to his previous luminous portrait of Mlle Shackleton.

Page 466, after "les plaisirs de la scène." A full paragraph describes Gide's first visit to the theatre. He was eight years old and most reluctant to go, preferring the circus, where he knew what to expect. His Rouen cousins insisted, and he was enchanted by "la biche au bois". He recalls everything, including his parents' concern because from their seats they had too good a view of the exuberant actresses' *décolletage.* Not in FE. Omitted perhaps as an excessive digression.

Page 469, after "de ce passé." A sentence explains that Madame de R. (de Witt) often took her meals alone; in any case, he has very little recollection of her being at the table at Val-Richer when he was there. Also in FE. Perhaps suppressed as being irrelevant.

Page 472, after "glané par ailleurs." A long sentence gives another example of Lionel's (François's) verbal plagiarism, in this case the repetition as his own of a comment about Dostoevsky which Gide had given him to read the previous evening. Not in FE. Probably suppressed for concision.

Page 472. In the MS the chronology of the relationship with Armand Bavretel is the reverse of what it is in the printed editions. Gide first wrote that he continued to go to see his friend for several years rather than several months. On page 477, he originally placed Bavretel's suicide as several months after their last meeting rather than several years. Changes made possibly in the interest of accuracy.

Chapter Seven

Page 478. The MS contains three separate notes which look like rejected beginnings to Chapter Seven. The first discusses in five sentences the bleakness which he finds dominating the account of his life up to this point. The second complains (in three sentences) that the period of his life which he is about to relate presents special problems, since he was at this point no longer a marionette, but not yet a fully developed personality. The third passage of five sentences contains a commentary on M. Richard's (Bauer's) move from Passy. None of these passages appear at the beginning of the chapter in the FE. Much of the substance of the third one, however, appears further on in the chapter.

Page 478. In the MS the canary lands on young Gide's "épaule" rather than his "casquette". FE has "casquette".

Page 482, after "la dédicace." An episode describing a typical visit of M. Estéoule of Toulouse to the Richard home. This pretentious but penniless tenor would not leave without a handout. Gide repeats a conversation with M. Richard after the visit, in which M. Richard explains that he could not help being generous, although he had at first been determined not to be exploited. Mme Richard encouraged young Gide in his scolding of her husband's weakness. Also in FE. Most likely suppressed later since this episode has very little to do with Bernard Tissaudier (Albert Jalaguier) or Adrien Giffard (Adolphe Werly), who were the subjects at hand. The passage is linked slightly to Tissaudier because he approved of Gide's policy of dismissing all ignorant people like Estéoule in his "Traité sur l'éducation".

Page 487. In the MS, Gide is seventeen years old at the time when Albert Démarest intercedes to help him gain access to his father's library. The age sixteen in printed editions makes Madame Gide seem slightly less impossible as a censor of her son's reading.

Chapter Eight

Page 496. Much of the section on the joys of reading and walking with Emmanuèle appears in two handwritten copies.
Page 507. At the end of the chapter, after a space of one-third of a page, Gide begins a section which seemed intended to explain how and why he and Pierre Louÿs began to drift apart. This sentence and a half are not in FE.

Chapter Nine

Page 507. The beginning of the chapter explaining the backtracking to 1884 is slightly longer in the MS, and one significant sentence, "Ce n'est pas un roman que j'écris," is crossed out. FE is the same as the Pléiade. The abridged version complies with Gide's concern about excessive commentary.
Page 516, after "temps d'y revenir." A long passage with a single stroke through it, and the word "supprimer" beside it. Here Gide speaks of his occasional regret at not having been encouraged by his mother to pursue a career as a pianist. He feels that he could have played Chopin in particular better than most professionals, since he respects the work as it was written more than displays of technical virtuosity. He concedes, though, that his nervousness on playing in public was probably alone sufficient to justify his mother's decision. Not in FE. Perhaps suppressed as being excessive commentary.
Page 516. Following the preceding MS passage, but *not* crossed out, are several pages on Marc de la Nux. He stresses de la Nux's stubbornness in refusing to continue teaching him after his mother discouraged a musical career for her son. He describes the unpleasant theory lessons with de la Nux's son, his friendship with the father — in particular, the latter's confessions of extreme timidity in playing at concerts. De la Nux became more and more a recluse, cutting down his piano class, and seeing only one person of his own generation — in order to play checkers. De la Nux's marital life is described with emphasis on his wife's duplicity in helping conceal their unmarried daughter's pregnancy from her father, and his firm rejection of

the daughter for fifteen years after he found out. The daughter still visited her mother, and when one day by accident de la Nux answered the door, he noticed that she had grey hair; but instead of a reconciliation after all these years, he chose to flee. It is one of her daughters (Mimi) who is mentioned at the bottom of Pléiade, page 517. He devoted all his affection to his grandchildren. The bulk of the passage is replaced in the FE by the shorter version which we find in the Pléiade (pp. 516-18). Gide offers the explanation on page 517 that he was afraid of overloading his work with stories of Marc de la Nux. (The story of the daughter would seem to have been in part a source for Gide's *Isabelle*.)

Page 519, after "que je la dois." The paragraph continues at some length to acknowledge Gide's indebtedness to foreign influences: Heine, Poe, Tourgueneff, and Schopenhauer in his youth; Goethe and Dostoevsky later; and, of course, Chopin. He reiterates his opinion that the French mind is suitable for digesting foreign influences, and that his in particular could have even digested pebbles! Also in FE. Perhaps suppressed as excessive and redundant commentary. He had already expressed these ideas elsewhere.

Page 520, after "et sans compagnon." A sentence explains that a blank spot on the map of Brittany rather similar to the unexplored areas of the African interior tempted him in his itinerary. Not in FE.

Page 520, after "sans intérêt." A comment of two short sentences explains that Gide still felt at the time of writing *Si le grain ne meurt* that his *Notes sur un voyage en Bretagne* were uninteresting; nevertheless, "Ces pages forment à proprement parler mon opus I." Not in FE. Suppressed commentary.

Page 520. In both the MS and FE it is beer and not cider which Gide is drinking; and the stopping-point which he rejects reaching that night is Hennebon rather than Pont-Aven.

Page 521. On the *verso* of MS γ 886-H118 is an *ébauche* for *Les Faux-monnayeurs* which gives ample evidence of the closeness in time of composition of the two works:

> Papiers d'Edouard
> Lettre à X. "Certes, il eu [*sic*] beau de libérer des
> esclaves. Mais l'emploi de leur liberté
> reconquise — c'est ceci qui m'intéresse.

Page 525. In the MS there are several very repetitive versions of the explanation of his attitude towards success. (The length of time he spent writing of his relative lack of concern for immediate public acclaim merely serves to cast doubt on his sincerity. His attitude seems to have developed out of necessity rather than from a retiring nature; and the examples of late adulation which developed for authors like Stendhal proved to be useful psychological support in the face of his disappointment.) FE is for the most part like the Pléiade here.

Page 527. In the MS, the section γ 886-N176-180 bears the general heading "La Cousine de Feuchères". There are minor stylistic variants throughout the whole episode, but one of special interest is that after "bonnet de dentelle" (p. 529), the MS has, "comme en portaient aussi ma mère ou Anna." Not in FE. This omission gives the lady's costume a more extraordinary effect than the comparison would allow.

Chapter Ten

From this point on, the manuscript in the Bibliothèque Doucet is fragmentary. Where the MS is missing, collating has been between the First Edition and the Pléiade.

Page 547. The note, after "simultanéité confuse." Both the MS and FE continue: "Je dirais volontiers de moi ce qu'écrivait Fénelon: 'Je ne puis expliquer mon fond. Il m'échappe et me paraît changer à toute heure. Je ne saurais guère rien dire qui ne me paraisse faux un moment après.'" The MS gives the bibliographical source in Fénelon, which the FE omits: "(*Lettres spirituelles*, p. 167, Hachette)". The note in the MS concludes with a mention of his lack of curiosity about the opposite sex. This suggests that at one time the note was meant to be incorporated in the regular text related particularly (perhaps as a transition into Part Two) to the question of homosexuality. FE concludes as in the Pléiade.

Chapter One

Page 549. Part Two in the FE is prefaced with the quote from Fénelon. In this edition, then, it was used twice, whereas in the Pléiade it appears not at all. The full quote is as follows: "Je tiens à tout d'une certaine façon, et cela est incroyable; mais d'une autre façon, j'y tiens peu, car je me laisse assez facilement détacher de la plupart des choses qui peuvent me flatter. Je n'en sens pas moins l'attachement foncier à moi-même. Au reste je ne puis expliquer mon fond. Il m'échappe, il me paraît changer à toute heure. Je ne saurais guère rien dire qui ne me paraisse faux un moment après. — Fénelon, *Lettres spirituelles,* p. 167." In a letter dated October 20, 1920, Gide asked Martin du Gard to identify the author of this passage. Its content and style suggested at once André Gide. (*Correspondance, André Gide-Roger Martin du Gard*, I: 160).

Page 555, after "Biskra par le sud." In the MS this sentence continues with the observation that quite naïvely the travellers were not taking into account the possibility of inclement weather, fearing only the heat. Also in FE. The revised version is more succinct, and just as clear.

Page 557, after "le moyen de refuser?" A sentence saying that Laurens and Gide persevered in refusing to move from the village to the camp, until a second spahi came to insist. Also in FE. Perhaps suppressed for concision.

Page 559, after "alla quérir un médecin." A parenthesis to the effect that for once the letters of reference were useful—in summoning a doctor. Also in FE. (The letter of introduction had already appeared in Chapter One of *L'Immoraliste*.)

Page 561, after "la marque de mon délire". Direct discourse of Paul Laurens exclaiming that on his return from his adventure, Gide resembled Bacchus; but in spite of Laurens's suspicions, Gide told him nothing of his very recent pleasure. Not in FE. At the end of this section in the MS, there is a paragraph marked "à réserver" which says, in essence, that while many people might wish for him (Gide) to say that after this sexual experience he had felt remorseful, he had in fact felt nothing of the kind.

Page 562, after "avec les pensionnaires de l'hôtel." A short passage with a blue line through it indicates that throughout this trip the state of his health forced him to take his meals apart from the others, as the long *tables d'hôte* caused him excruciating discomfort. Not in FE. Perhaps omitted as being non-essential.

Page 563. A footnote pendent on "d'autre société que la leur." In this note Gide attempts to justify his not having visited the Ben-Ganah, a breach of etiquette which had resulted in subsequent criticism. In 1893 his poor health had prevented the visit, and on his second trip to Biskra he was determined to frequent only the "low people". Also in FE. Later omitted, as passing time had most likely minimized the importance of his social gaffe.

Page 572, after "qu'à Cuverville". The FE continues "ou à Yport". Later omitted when Gide recalled more definitely the place of his reunion with Laurens.

Page 573, after "s'écria Hérold." In the FE, a sentence in parentheses states that he has already said that Hérold needed constant companionship. Doubtless omitted as a superfluous repetition.

Page 574. Of the two footnotes, only the second is in the FE. The footnote on page 582 does not appear in the FE either.

Page 577, after "que dorait l'automne." The FE continues with thoughts on the regrettable construction work which has spoiled so many of the landscapes which were beautiful in his childhood. Perhaps omitted as excessive commentary.

Page 577. In the FE the verb accompanying "Cet inquiet démon" is "possédait" rather than "tourmentait". The later version ("tourmentait") consi: lerably lessens the demon's power over him.

Chapter Two

Page 589, after "plus le revoir." In the FE, Wilde's discourse is continued with the unnecessary explanation: "Vous comprenez, n'est-ce pas, que ce n'est pas la même chose."

Page 589. In the FE the location where the taxi dropped Wilde and Gide was described not as the rue Montpensier, but "la troisième terrasse des rampes Rovigo".

Page 594, after "simplement ma mesure". In the FE there is the apologetic remark in parentheses: "(j'entends: celle des meilleurs jours)". Doubtless omitted because the parenthesis invites distracting speculation about Gide's honesty here.

Page 596, after "ou des chats." In the FE the sentence continues, "ou que l'onanisme des poissons."

Page 612, after "une sorte d'abnégation capiteuse." In the FE the sentence continues with a confession about the complacency of Gide's abnegation. Omitted probably because of redundancy.

REPENTIRS

The manuscript contains several "repentirs" in addition to the Gérardmer envelope mentioned previously. Four of them are grouped under the general number y886-B2-5 in the Bibliothèque Doucet.

The first one appears to have been meant to introduce Part Two. It throws light on Gide's concern for presenting events just as they appeared to him when he was experiencing them. For this reason, he says, he has rejected the idea of presenting the devil ("le Malin") in the early part, since it was actually some time before he recognized who his adversary was. He has often wished that he could meet the adolescent he used to be, although he recognizes that the two selves would not mix well. The boy would be afraid of the adult, and the adult would wish to disengage the boy from his virtuous ideals. The desire to corrupt the virtuous, he observes, is one of the accoutrements of vice, whose chains have supplanted those of virtue in his life, and in fact have proven to be even more binding.

A second *repentir* briefly draws attention to how limited his early recollections seem in comparison with the profusion of those for the later period.

The third *repentir* would seem to have been written after the first eight chapters had gone to press, but while he was still writing the remaining parts. He seems to have come to realize that the real division in his life does not fall between the eighth and the ninth chapters, but rather with his first trip to Africa in 1893. The intervening period gives him trouble because of the formlessness which his character took at that time, a formlessness brought about by his attraction to lofty aspirations and extraordinary abnegation.

A fourth *repentir* begins by emphasizing how difficult it would have been for him to free himself from his dedication to virtue. He goes on to say that he believes that it was his passion to overcome the difficult which influenced him to strive so stubbornly; but it is not clear whether the object of his efforts here is virtue or, on the contrary, liberation from its constraint. He admits that the act of liberating himself from the ties of virtue would at this point have been more difficult for him than the attainment of ideal purity.

A brief *repentir*, filed as γ 886-P 186, would seem to be linked with Gide's departure for Africa. He states that his few earlier trips to Holland, Brittany, and Spain appeared to him as merely preparatory. On the same page, he states that all his works but *Isabelle* have been dictated by the needs of his heart.

Bibliography

I MANUSCRIPT

There is evidence that further pertinent manuscripts are extant. Jean Delay speaks of consulting the preparatory notes which Gide collected, and the catalogue of the 1970 Bibliothèque Nationale exhibition on Gide (p. 151) mentions some items from this dossier (entitled here *De me ipse*) lent from a private collection. The same catalogue (p. 152) mentions five hand-written notebooks containing "la version définitive" of the text — also from a private collection. These documents remain inaccessible to most scholars in the field.

I describe the Bibliothèque Doucet manuscript as it appears in that library's catalogue — in French. Also included here is the recently unearthed *inédit* mentioned in Chapter IV *supra*.

GIDE, ANDRÉ. *Si le grain ne meurt*. Manuscrit autographe, sans lieu ni date [sauf certains feuillets]. Formats divers, 447 feuillets y compris des "repentirs", tous classées en 31 fascicules. Certaines parties du texte manquent à ce manuscrit. Paris: Bibliothèque Jacques Doucet. Cote générale, γ 886.

_____. "Une page inédite de *Si le grain ne meurt*". *Le Républicain d'Uzès et du Gard*, le 19 juillet 1969, pp. 1-2.

II EDITIONS OF "SI LE GRAIN NE MEURT"

A. Earliest Editions

For further data consult Arnold Naville, *Bibliographie des écrits d'André Gide* (Paris: Matarasso, 1949).

113

GIDE, ANDRÉ. *"Si le grain ne meurt*. Fragments.*" Nouvelle Revue Française*, 7ᵉ année, février, mars, mai, novembre, décembre, 1920; 8ᵉ année, janvier 1921; 11ᵉ année, janvier 1924. "Edition préoriginale".

———. *Si le grain ne meurt*. Paris: Sans nom d'éditeur [Bruges: Imprimerie Sainte-Catherine]. [Achevé d'imprimer le 15 mai] 1920. Hors commerce—12 exemplaires. "Edition originale" de la Première Partie, Chapitres 1-8.

———. *Si le grain ne meurt*, Deuxième Volume. Paris: Sans nom d'éditeur [Bruges: Imprimerie Sainte-Catherine]. [Achevé d'imprimer le 24 décembre] 1921. Hors commerce—13 exemplaires. "Edition originale" de la Première Partie, Chapitres 9-10, et de la Deuxième Partie.

———. "Hérédité." In *Morceaux choisis*. Paris: Nouvelle Revue Française, 1921.

———. *André Gide* [*Pages choisies*]. Paris: G. Crès et Cie., Bibliothèque de l'Adolescence, sans date [1921]. Extraits des trois premiers chapitres. Quelques tirages portent le sous-titre "Romans et essais".

———. "Préface" à Robert Doré et Raoul Simonson, *Les Livres d'André Gide*. Paris: Edouard Champion, 1923. Fragment du Chapitre 9.

———. *Fragment de "Si le grain ne meurt"*. Sans lieu, sans nom d'éditeur, sans date [Paris: Edouard Champion, 1924]. Réproduction en phototypie du Chapitre 10 (manuscrit autographe).

———. *Si le grain ne meurt: Souvenirs d'enfance et de jeunesse*. Oxford: Clarendon Press, 1925. Fragments édités par V. F. Boyson, avec un avant-propos d'André Gide. "Edition classique anglaise": fragments des trois premiers chapitres.

———. *Si le grain ne meurt*. 3 vols. Paris: Nouvelle Revue Française, 1924. "Nouvelle édition"; première édition intégrale dans le commerce; mise en vente, 1926.

———. *Si le grain ne meurt*. Paris: Nouvelle Revue Française, 1928. "Edition courante"; mise en vente, 1929.

B. Standard Current Editions

GIDE, ANDRÉ. *"Si le grain ne meurt"*. In *Journal 1939-1949; Souvenirs*, pp. 347-615. Paris: Gallimard, Bibliothèque de la Pléiade, 1954.

BIBLIOGRAPHY

_____. *Si le grain ne meurt*. Paris: Livre de poche, 1966.

_____. *Si le grain ne meurt*. Paris: Gallimard, Collection Folio 96, 1972.

III EDITIONS OF OTHER WORKS BY ANDRÉ GIDE CITED

GIDE, ANDRÉ. *Les Cahiers et les poésies d'André Walter*. Paris: Gallimard, 1952.

_____. *Dostoïevski*. Paris: Gallimard, Collection Idées, 1964.

_____. *Incidences*. Paris: Gallimard, 1951.

_____. *Journal 1889-1939*. Paris: Gallimard, Bibliothèque de la Pléiade, 1951.

_____. *Journal des Faux-monnayeurs*. Paris: Gallimard, 1951.

_____. *Oeuvres complètes*. 15 vols. Paris: Gallimard, 1932-39.

_____. *Romans; Récits et soties; Oeuvres lyriques*. Paris: Gallimard, Bibliothèque de la Pléiade, 1958.

_____, et DU BOS, CHARLES. *Lettres de Charles Du Bos et réponses d'André Gide*. Paris: Corrêa, 1950.

_____, and GOSSE, EDMUND. *The Correspondence of André Gide and Edmund Gosse, 1904-1928*. Edited with translation, introduction, and notes by Linette F. Brugmans. London: Peter Owen, 1960.

_____, et MARTIN DU GARD, ROGER. *Correspondance André Gide—Roger Martin du Gard, 1913-1951*. Introduction par Jean Delay. 2 vols. Paris: Gallimard, 1968.

_____, et MAURIAC, FRANÇOIS. *Correspondance André Gide—François Mauriac, 1912-1950*. Edition établie, présentée, et annotée par Jacqueline Morton. *Cahiers André Gide*, 2. Paris: Gallimard, 1971.

_____, et VALÉRY, PAUL. *Correspondance André Gide—Paul Valéry, 1890-1942*. Préface et notes par Robert Mallet. Paris: Gallimard, 1955.

IV STUDIES DEVOTED IN WHOLE OR IN PART
     TO "SI LE GRAIN NE MEURT"

This list includes early reviews, as well as articles and books. Almost all the standard surveys of Gide's career contain at least a few paragraphs on *Si le grain ne meurt*. They have been generally omitted here.

BERNARD, GUY. "Divers". *La Revue Nouvelle,* le 15 février 1927, pp. 55-6.

BERTAUX, FÉLIX. *"Si le grain ne meurt"*. *Nouvelle Revue Française*, 14ᵉ année, février 1927, pp. 258-63.

BOISDEFFRE, PIERRE DE. *Vie d'André Gide 1869-1951: Essai de biographie critique.* Vol. I: *André Gide avant la fondation de la "Nouvelle Revue Française" (1869-1909).* Paris: Hachette, 1970.

CASSOU, JEAN. *"Si no muere el grano".* La Gaceta Literaria, 15 mai, 1927.

CHAPON, FRANÇOIS. "Note sur l'édition du second *Corydon".* Bulletin du Bibliophile I (1971): 1-9.

DELAY, JEAN. *La Jeunesse d'André Gide.* 2 vols. Paris: Gallimard, 1956-7.

DU BOS, CHARLES. *Le Dialogue avec André Gide.* Paris: Au Sans Pareil, 1929.

GOURMONT, JEAN DE. *"Si le grain ne meurt".* Mercure de France, le 1er mars 1927, pp. 388-91.

HOY, PETER C. "From André Gide to Edmund Gosse". *American Notes and Queries*, n.s., II (November 1963): 36-8.

_____. "R. Harborough Sherard, Lord Alfred Douglas, and André Gide's *Si le grain ne meurt".* Adam, nos. 337-9 (1970), pp. 52-61.

IRELAND, G. W. *André Gide: A Study of His Creative Writings.* Oxford: Clarendon Press, 1970. (See Chapter 22, "Personal Writings", pp. 326-39.)

LALOU, RENÉ. "Lettres parisiennes, XIII". *Het Fransche Boek*, April 1927, pp. 113-15.

LEJEUNE, PHILIPPE. *Exercices d'ambiguité: Lectures de "Si le grain ne meurt" d'André Gide.* Paris: Lettres Modernes, 1974.

_____. "Gide et l'autobiographie", *André Gide*, 4. Paris: Minard, La Revue des Lettres Modernes, 1974.

MARLOW, GEORGES. *"Si le grain ne meurt,* de M. André Gide", *Le Thyrse*, 29e année, no. 8 (le 20 février 1927), pp. 85-8.

MARTIN DU GARD, MAURICE. "P.S." *Les Nouvelles Littéraires*, le 4 décembre 1926.

MOUTOTE, DANIEL. *Le "Journal" de Gide et les problèmes du moi (1889-1925).* Paris: Presses Universitaires de France, 1968.

SHERARD, ROBERT HARBOROUGH. *André Gide's Wicked Lies about the late Mr. Oscar Wilde in Algiers in January, 1895.* Calvi: Vindex, 1933.

SOUDAY, PAUL. "Les Livres". *Le Temps*, le 23 décembre 1926.

VANDEREM, FERNAND. "Les Lettres et la vie". *La Revue de France*, le 15 décembre 1926, pp. 733-8.

BIBLIOGRAPHY
V   A SELECTION OF OTHER RELEVANT
       STUDIES ON ANDRÉ GIDE

BORNECQUE, J. HENRY. "André Gide et *Du côté de chez Swann*". *Bulletin de la Société des Amis de Marcel Proust et des Amis de Combray*, no. 7 (1957), pp. 307-9.

BRÉE, GERMAINE. *André Gide, l'insaisissable Protée*. Paris: Société édition des Belles-lettres, 1953.

BRENNER, JACQUES. "Le Péché d'inexactitude". *Cahiers des Saisons*, no. 17 (été 1959), pp. 163-5.

COLLET, GEORGES-PAUL. "André Gide épistolier". In *Entretiens sur André Gide*, pp. 69-79. Sous la direction de Marcel Arland et Jean Mouton. La Haye: Mouton, 1967.

COLLIGNON, JEAN. "Gide's Sincerity". *Yale French Studies*, no. 7 (1951), pp. 44-50.

COTNAM, JACQUES. "Le *Subjectif* ou les lectures d'André Gide (1889-1893)". In *Cahiers André Gide*, 1, pp. 15-113. Paris: Gallimard, 1969.

DELAY, JEAN. "Gide ou l'expérience de soi". In *Cahiers André Gide*, 3, pp. 81-91. Paris: Gallimard, 1972.

DERAIS, FRANÇOIS, et RAMBAUD, HENRI. *L'Envers du "Journal" de Gide*. Paris: Le Nouveau Portique, 1952.

ETIEMBLE. "Les Artifices ou non de l'écriture". In *Cahiers André Gide*, 3, pp. 155-62. Paris: Gallimard, 1972.

GHIASSI, MOHAMMED-TAGHI. "L'Influence de Stendhal sur André Gide: Etude historique". Doctoral thesis, Université de Paris, 1964.

GIRARD, ALAIN. "Le *Journal* dans l'oeuvre de Gide". In *Entretiens sur André Gide*, pp. 183-97. Sous la direction de Marcel Arland et Jean Mouton. La Haye: Mouton, 1967.

GOULET, ALAIN. "Les Premiers Vers d'André Gide (1888-1891)". In *Cahiers André Gide*, 1, pp. 123-49. Paris: Gallimard, 1969.

GUILLEMIN, HENRI. "A propos du *Journal* d'André Gide". In *A vrai dire*, pp. 211-13. Paris: Gallimard, 1956.

HOLDHEIM, W. WOLFGANG. *Theory and Practice of the Novel: A Study on André Gide*. Geneva: Droz, 1968.

KNIGHT, EVERETT. "Stendhal et André Gide". *French Review* XXIV (May 1951): 461-70.

LAFILLE, PIERRE. *André Gide romancier*. Paris: Hachette, 1954.

LAMBINET, MARIE-THÉRÈSE. "André Gide et le roman". *Marche Romane* IX (avril-juin 1959): 75-83.

MARTIN, CLAUDE. *André Gide par lui-même*. Paris: Aux Editions du Seuil, 1962.

_____. "Une Conclusion aux *Faux-monnayeurs*". *Bulletin des Lettres*, 19ᵉ année, no. 186 (le 15 mars 1927), pp. 89-94.

_____. "Etat présent des études gidiennes 1951-1963". *Critique* XX (juillet 1964): 598-625.

_____. "Toujours vivant, toujours secret". *Etudes Littéraires* II (décembre 1969): 289-303.

MARTIN-CHAUFFIER, LOUIS. "Un Génie de la contradiction". *Le Figaro Littéraire*, le 18 août 1969, pp. 4-6.

MARTIN DU GARD, ROGER. *Oeuvres complètes*. 2 vols. Paris: Gallimard, Bibliothèque de la Pléiade, 1955.
(See the *Notes sur André Gide,* vol. II, pp. 1355-1423.)

MATTHEISEN, PAUL F. "More on Gosse and Gide". *Notes and Queries*, n.s., X (October 1963): 377-79.

MICHAUD, GUY. *L'Oeuvre et ses techniques*. Paris: Nizet, 1957.
(See the "Genèse des *Faux-monnayeurs*", pp. 152-63.)

NAIRNE, CAMPBELL. "The Novels of André Gide". *The Listener,* October 21, 1948, p. 608.

NOBÉCOURT, R.-G. *Les Nourritures normandes d'André Gide*. Paris: Editions Médicis, 1949.

O'BRIEN, JUSTIN. "Additions to the Gide Bibliography". In *Contemporary French Literature*. Edited and introduced by Leon S. Roudiez. New Brunswick, N.J.: Rutgers University Press, 1971.

_____. *Portrait of André Gide*. London: Secker and Warburg, 1953.

PAINTER, GEORGE D. *André Gide: A Critical Biography*. London: Weidenfeld and Nicolson, 1968.

_____. "The Novels of André Gide". *The Listener*, October 14, 1948, pp. 573-4, and October 28, 1948, p. 649.

PEYRE, HENRI. "André Gide et les problèmes d'influence en littérature". *Modern Language Notes* LVII (November 1942): 558-67.

RAMBAUD, HENRI. "La Phrase de Madeleine". In *Cahiers André Gide*, 1, pp. 319-70. Paris: Gallimard, 1969.

SCHLUMBERGER, JEAN. *Madeleine et André Gide*. Paris: Gallimard, 1956.

STARKIE, ENID. *André Gide*. Cambridge: Bowes and Bowes, 1953.

STEEL, D. A. "Gide à l'école de Stendhal: Le Héros illégitime". *Essays in French Literature*, no. 4 (November 1967): 30-43.

STRAUSS, GEORGE. "Le Thème des soeurs dans l'oeuvre d'André Gide". In *Cahiers André Gide*, 1, pp. 241-64. Paris: Gallimard, 1969.

VAN RYSSELBERGHE, MARIA. *Les Cahiers de la Petite Dame: Notes pour l'histoire authentique d'André Gide, 1918-29*. *Cahiers André Gide*, 4. Paris: Gallimard, 1973.

VILDÉ-LOT, IRÈNE. "André Gide et l'art d'écrire d'après les variantes des *Nourritures terrestres* et de quelques autres oeuvres de jeunesse". *Le Français Moderne* XXVIII (1960): 259-68; XXIX (1961): 29-42, 121-83, 206-22.

WEINBERG, KURT. *On Gide's "Prométhée": Private Myth and Public Mystification*. Princeton, N.J.: Princeton University Press, 1972.

YOURCENAR, MARGUERITE. "André Gide Revisited". In *Cahiers André Gide*, 3, pp. 21-44. Paris: Gallimard, 1972.

VI STUDIES ON THE THEORY, HISTORY, OR ART OF AUTOBIOGRAPHY

BOISDEFFRE, PIERRE DE. "Renouvellement du roman français par l'autobiographie". In *Positions et oppositions sur le roman contemporain: Actes du Colloque de Strasbourg*, pp. 63-78. Paris: Klincksieck, 1971.

BOOTH, WAYNE C. *The Rhetoric of Fiction*. Chicago: University of Chicago Press, 1961.

BOREL, JACQUES. "Problèmes de l'autobiographie". In *Positions et oppositions sur le roman contemporain: Actes du Colloque de Strasbourg*, pp. 79-90. Paris: Klincksieck, 1971.

COURCELLE, PIERRE. *Les "Confessions" de Saint-Augustin dans la tradition littéraire, antécédents et postérité*. Paris: Etudes augustiniennes, 1963.

DOBRÉE, BONAMY. "Some Literary Autobiographies of the Present Age". *The Sewanee Review* LXIV (Autumn 1956): 689-706.

FERNANDEZ, RAMON. "L'Autobiographie et le roman. L'Exemple de Stendhal". In *Messages*, pp. 79-109. Paris: Gallimard, 1926.

FRIEDMAN, NORMAN. "Point of View in Fiction: The Development of a Critical Concept". *PMLA* LXX (December 1955): 1160-84.

GUSDORF, GEORGES. "Conditions et limites de l'autobiographie". In *Festgabe für Fritz Neubert: Formen der Selbstdarstellung*, pp. 105-23. Berlin: Duncker und Humblot, 1956.

———. *La Découverte de soi*. Paris: Presses Universitaires de France, 1948.

JONES, P. MANSELL. *French Introspectives from Montaigne to André Gide*. Cambridge: Cambridge University Press, 1937.

LEJEUNE, PHILIPPE. *L'Autobiographie en France*. Paris: Armand Colin, Collection U2, 1971.

———. "Le Pacte autobiographique". *Poétique*, no. 14 (1973), pp. 137-62.

LILLARD, RICHARD G. *American Life in Autobiography: A Descriptive Guide*. Stanford: Stanford University Press, 1956.

LOBET, MARCEL. *Ecrivains en aveu, essai sur la confession littéraire*. Paris: Garnier, 1962.

MAUROIS, ANDRÉ. *Aspects de la biographie*. Paris: Grasset, 1928. (See Chapter 5, "L'Autobiographie", pp. 129-55.)

MAZLISH, BRUCE. "Autobiography and Psychoanalysis". *Encounter*, October 1970, pp. 28-37.

MISCH, GEORG. *A History of Autobiography in Antiquity*. 2 vols. London: Routledge and Kegan Paul, 1950.

MORRIS, JOHN N. *Versions of the Self: Studies in English Autobiography from John Bunyan to John Stuart Mill*. New York and London: Basic Books, 1966.

OLNEY, JAMES. *Metaphors of Self: The Meaning of Autobiography*. Princeton, N.J.: Princeton University Press, 1972.

PASCAL, ROY. "The Autobiographical Novel and the Autobiography", *Essays in Criticism* IX (April 1959): 134-50.

———. *Design and Truth in Autobiography*. London: Routledge and Kegan Paul, 1960.

PEYRE, HENRI. *Literature and Sincerity*. New Haven, Conn.: Yale University Press, 1963. (See especially Chapter 9, "André Gide: Martyr and Hero of Sincerity", pp. 276-305.)

POUILLON, JEAN. *Temps et roman*. Paris: Gallimard, 1946. (See "L'Autobiographie", pp. 52-68.)

POULET, ROBERT. "Sur la littérature personnelle". *Ecrits de Paris*, mars 1970, pp. 92-9.

ROMBERG, BERTIL. *Studies in the Narrative Technique in the First-Person Novel*. Stockholm: Almqvist and Wiksell, 1962.

SHAPIRO, STEPHEN A. "The Dark Continent of Literature: Autobiography". *Comparative Literature Studies* V (December 1968): 421-54.

SHUMAKER, WAYNE. *English Autobiography: Its Emergence, Materials, and Form*. Berkeley and Los Angeles: University of California Press, 1954.

SPENDER, STEPHEN. "Confessions and Autobiography". In *The Making of a Poem*, pp. 63-72. London: Hamish Hamilton, 1955.

STAROBINSKI, JEAN. "Le Style de l'autobiographie". *Poétique*, no. 3 (1970), pp. 257-65.

STEPHEN, LESLIE. "Autobiography". In *Hours in a Library*, vol. III, pp. 237-70. London: Smith, Elder, 1892.

TRILLING, LIONEL. *Sincerity and Authenticity*. Cambridge, Mass.: Harvard University Press, 1973.

VOISINE, JACQUES. "Naissance et évolution du terme littéraire 'autobiographie'". In *La Littérature comparée en Europe orientale, conférence de Budapest, 26-29 octobre 1962*, pp. 278-86. Budapest: Akadémiai Kiadó, 1963.

WETHERED, H. N. *The Curious Art of Autobiography from Benvenuto Cellini to Rudyard Kipling*. New York: Philosophical Library, 1956.

VII OTHER WORKS CITED

ALAIN. "Autobiographie". *La Table Ronde*, no. 89 (mai 1955), pp. 77-82.

ALAIN-FOURNIER. *Le Grand Meaulnes*. Paris: Livre de poche, 1963.

ALBALAT, ANTOINE. *Le Travail du style enseigné par les corrections manuscrites des grands écrivains*. Paris: Armand Colin, 1903.

AXTHELM, PETER M. *The Modern Confessional Novel*. New Haven, Conn.: Yale University Press, 1967.

BROWN, E. K. *Rhythm in the Novel*. Toronto: University of Toronto Press, 1957.

CAMUS, ALBERT. *La Chute*. Paris: Gallimard, 1956.

DUCHÊNE, ROGER. "Réalité vécue et réussite littéraire: Le Statut particulier de la lettre". *Revue d'Histoire Littéraire de la France*, 71ᵉ année, no. 2 (mars-avril 1971), pp. 177-94.

FRANCE, ANATOLE. *La Vie littéraire*, 1ère série. Paris: Calmann-Lévy, 1888.

FROHOCK, W. M. *Style and Temper: Studies in French Fiction 1925-1960*. Oxford: Blackwell, 1967.

GIRARD, ALAIN. *Le Journal intime*. Paris: Presses Universitaires de France, 1963.

GOSSE, EDMUND. *Father and Son: A Study of Two Temperaments*. London: Heinemann, 1930.

LAVONDÈS, A. *Charles Gide*. Uzès: La Capitelle, 1953.

LE VERDIER, PIERRE. *Une Famille de haute bourgeoisie rouennaise: Histoire de la famille Rondeaux*. Rouen: Imprimerie Cagniard, 1928.

MAURIAC, FRANÇOIS. *Commencements d'une vie*. Paris: Grasset, 1932.

PAINTER, GEORGE D. *Marcel Proust: A Biography*. 2 vols. London: Chatto and Windus, 1966.

PRAZ, MARIO. *The Romantic Agony*. 2nd ed. London: Oxford University Press, 1951.

PRÉVOST, JEAN. *La Création chez Stendhal*. Paris: Mercure de France, 1951.

PROUST, MARCEL. *A la recherche du temps perdu*. 8 vols. Paris: Livre de poche, 1965-67.

RUFENACHT, CHARLES. *Michel de la Roche (1775-1852): Ses Aïeux et ses ascendants*. Le Havre: Hors commerce, 1963.

SARTRE, JEAN-PAUL. "Jean-Paul Sartre on his Autobiography: An Interview with Olivier Todd". *The Listener,* June 6, 1957, pp. 915-16.

———. *Les Mots*. Paris: Gallimard, 1964.

STENDHAL. *La Chartreuse de Parme*. Paris: Garnier, 1961.

———. *Vie de Henry Brulard*. Paris: Garnier, 1961.

WELLEK, RENÉ, and WARREN, AUSTIN. *Theory of Literature*. New York: Harcourt, Brace, 1949.